LOST

Cathy Ostlere

Lost

A MEMOIR

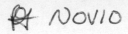

KEY PORTER BOOKS

Library and Archives Canada Cataloguing in Publication

Ostlere, Cathy
   Lost : a memoir / Cathy Ostlere.

ISBN 978-1-55470-043-1

   1. Ostlere, Cathy--Family. 2. Ostlere, David-- Death. I. Title.

PS8629.S57L67 2008   C813'.6   C2007-905478-1

 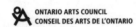

The publisher gratefully acknowledges the support of the Canada Council for the Arts and the Ontario Arts Council for its publishing program. We acknowledge the support of the Government of Ontario through the Ontario Media Development Corporation's Ontario Book Initiative.

We acknowledge the financial support of the Government of Canada through the Book Publishing Industry Development Program (BPIDP) for our publishing activities.

Key Porter Books Limited
Six Adelaide Street East, Tenth Floor
Toronto, Ontario
Canada M5C 1H6

www.keyporter.com
Author's Website: www.cathy-ostlere.com

Electronic formatting: Jean Lightfoot Peters

Printed and bound in Canada

08 09 10 11 12 5 4 3 2 1

There is so little to remember of anyone—an anecdote, a conversation at table. But every memory is turned over and over again, every word, however chance, written in the heart in the hope that memory will fulfill itself, and become flesh, and that the wanderers will find a way home, and the perished, whose lack we always feel, will step through the door finally and stroke our hair with dreaming, habitual fondness, not having meant to keep us waiting long.

MARILYNNE ROBINSON
Housekeeping

The water remembers what happened to the ship.

PABLO NERUDA
The Magellan Heart (1519)

For my children

In memory of David Ostlere and Sarah Heald

ACKNOWLEDGEMENTS

SO MANY WANTED THIS story to be told and I thank the friends and strangers who listened, encouraged, and offered their own memories.

Special thanks to my parents, and my sister and brother, who accepted my desire to tell this story in my own way. Their respect and trust is humbly appreciated.

To Sarah's family, deepest gratitude for generosity in the midst of their own grieving. Thanks to Heather and Derek for their grace, Xanthe who calmed my sadness, and in memory of Richard who taught me that a time comes when we must let go.

Thanks to Jo Buckle, a guardian angel who unreservedly helped a stranger in need, and to Mr. Luis Filip Vidigal Aragão, for his patience and support. Appreciation to Jaoa Campelo Fernandez, David Lumby and Nick. Thanks also to the British Coastguard in Falmouth, U.K., particularly Steven Huxley. I would like to extend my gratitude to the Irish community of Castletownbere that showed me such warmth and kindness, especially Margaret, Anne, Ellen, Niall, and the magnificent Adrienne MacCarthy. To the people of Fionnphort, Scotland, thank you for your stories of David and Sarah. Special appreciation to Suzie, Carol, Ralph, Chris, Camilla, Nigel, Rosie, Hickey, and Peter Millar of the Iona Abbey. In memory of Andrew.

Much of this book was shaped and inspired by mentors at The Banff Centre. I am indebted to Sharon Butala who first read the opening scene (and seven years later the last), to Greg Hollingshead for constructive and sensitive criticism, and Edna Alford for unparalleled enthusiasm. Thanks to the other participants of the 2002 Writing Studio, particularly Maria Francesca LoDico. And thanks to Trevor Ferguson for friendship.

Gracious appreciation to Karen Connelly, my editor and mentor at the Humber School of Writing, and a most interesting friend.

Many writers kept this book moving forward. Heartfelt thanks to Marika Deliyannides and Natalee Caple for astute editing, Maria Smythe for faith, dee Hobsbawn-Smith for her poet's ear, Wade Bell for gentle encouragement, and Catherine Simmons for wisdom. Thanks also to Moe Gab and Michael Weaver. To Andrea Davies for her unwavering belief and so much more, and to Roberta Rees, teacher and friend extraordinaire, my deepest gratitude.

Much appreciation to the friends who were also readers: Lori Goldman, Barb Jessiman, Sarah Wilson and Pam Sullivan. To the *Minds Not Dryers Book Club*, I am most grateful for the inspiration, laughter and food. Thanks to former MP Jan Brown for assistance in the fall of 1995. For their nautical advice, thanks to Tony and Arien Knight who crossed the same waters on the *Ocean Wanderer* shortly after David and Sarah. I am also grateful to Mary Graham for assistance, and to Leda and Mark who enrich my life. Thanks to Larry Kirshbaum who cared about the story.

Portions of this book have appeared in *Event* and *Prairie Fire* magazines. My appreciation to the editors for their enthusiasm and interest.

Grateful acknowledgment is extended to the Canada Council and the Alberta Foundation for the Arts for the writing grants that supported this work.

To the staff at Key Porter, my gratitude and admiration for your work with *Lost*, especially to Sara Chappel, Jennifer Fox, Daniel Rondeau, Kelly Joseph, and Martin Gould.

To my delightful agent, John Pearce, with Westwood Creative Artists, many many thanks for taking a chance on *Lost*.

For Jonathan Schmidt, my editor at Key Porter, special thanks for extraordinary generosity. His faith, intelligence and deep understanding of the book was astonishing.

To T.G.W., for the loving acceptance and forgiveness, I am truly grateful.

And to Rand, thank you for the light.

Grateful acknowledgement is made to the following for permission to reproduce brief excerpts from the following copyrighted material:

Housekeeping by Marilynne Robinson. New York: Harper Collins Publishers, 1980 & 2004.

"The Magellan Heart (1519)" by Pablo Neruda. From *Selected Poems*, edited by Nathaniel Tarn. New York: Dell Publishing Company, 1970 & 1972.

"Whales Not Weep!" by D.H. Lawrence. From *The Complete Poems*. New York: Penguin Books, 1964 & 1993.

The Accidental Indies by Robert Finley. Montreal: McGill-Queen's University Press, 2000.

"The Comedian as the Letter C" by Wallace Stevens. From *The Collected Peoms of Wallace Stevens*. New York: Alfred A. Knopf, 1954 & 1989.

A River Runs Through It and Other Stories by Norman Maclean. New York: Pocket Books (Simon & Schuster Inc.), 1976 & 1992.

The Other Voice by Octavio Paz. Orlando: Harcourt Inc. 1990 & 1991.

"Homeward to Ithaca" by John Kincaid. From *From Windward to Ithaca: One Man's Love of Mull*. The Dorien Press, United Kingdom. 1986.

CONTENTS

I

II

I

For reasons of privacy, the names of some
individuals have been changed.

BIRTHDAY

A man sits as many risks as he runs.

HENRY DAVID THOREAU

WE SIT AROUND THE kitchen table, waiting.

A map of Vancouver Island floats under the glass-top table. My finger traces the west coastline of long deep inlets where rain in rivers is carried to a turgid sea. *Nootka, Esperanza, Quatsino.* My father sips loudly into his coffee cup. My mother clears her throat. Familiar habits. We are a prairie family—there is a certain dryness to us. When I lean over the table to look at Cape Scott, the point where the Pacific Ocean rounds the northern tip of the island, I accidentally knock over the saltshaker.

"It's the left shoulder," says my mother, but I leave the little crystals spilled. They catch the streams of the morning sun and glitter like quartz in sand. My mother pinches her fingertips together and flings the granules to the window. "We don't want any bad luck."

Today is my youngest brother's birthday. September 30, 1995. For the last seven years, David has telephoned from wherever he is in the world. He never forgets and neither do we. He sometimes calls each of us—my parents, a brother and sister in Winnipeg, and me in Calgary. We say happy birthday, our voices carried through deep cables across the ocean. In 1988, the year he met an Englishwoman named Sarah, he called from Brisbane, Australia. "We've sold the car and we're going to Japan." In 1990, he was in Guangzhou, China. This morning, my parents are expecting to hear his voice from a telephone booth in the south of England. But they will be mistaken. I am the only one in the family who knows that my brother and Sarah are headed to the open Atlantic. They plan to sail from Ireland to the Azores Archipelago and then on to the island of Madeira. By the end of today, I won't have to keep their secret any longer.

The waiting begins in the morning. Calgary is seven hours behind the U.K. We expect the call no later than noon. We root ourselves to the kitchen table. The Saturday newspaper is divided into sections: Spain is filing a suit against Canada over the turbot fish war, the Blue Bombers beat the Ticats. My husband Sam makes fresh coffee. Cold toast is replaced with warm buttery slices. The sun moves from behind the evergreens into the open sky and heats the kitchen. The air smells of browning apple peels. My three children graze, then spin off, dancing erratic orbits throughout the house. I am silent while staring at the excess of breakfast.

At ten, I lift the receiver to check for a dial tone, its comforting assurance of possibility. Who can I speak to?

"DON'T TELL ANYONE WHERE we're going," my brother entreats during a phone call last spring. "You know how Mom will be." I remember my own travels. She worried every minute.

"*Happiness is no way to live a life,*" I answer him jokingly. In a fit of frustration, our mother had once blurted out those words to us. We had laughed.

"If you would just stay home," she told us, "I wouldn't lose any sleep over the two of you."

Over the years David and I have learned that it's best not to tell our mother too much. Don't tell. Don't give too many details. Write often.

A letter in May 1983 began: *Dear David, It's true. The light is different in Greece. I am sailing on the* Lady Papillon, *a 38-foot sloop. We flew a spinnaker yesterday. It was yellow and thin as silk. It filled up like a heart. The captain is an Englishman named Simon.*

The children think there should be a birthday cake even if Uncle David isn't here. Coloured candles are tossed onto the table like runes. The wax is sticky and covered in crumbs just like the ones my mother keeps in her kitchen drawer. As a child I hated putting the used, unevenly melted candles into fresh soft icing, and yet now, I save the stumps too. After I've licked them.

"Don't we have any new ones that aren't deformed?" I ask. I roll a blue and white twist between my fingers. The thin black wick appears to go in and out like a tongue.

My mother flicks off the dried chunks of cake with her long, pink-coated thumbnail. "Oh, they're perfectly good, dear. David doesn't care about things like this."

"How old is he, Mommy?" Victoria, who's eight, is counting the candles.

"Thirty-six, sweetie."

"Thirty-five," my father corrects.

"Thirty-six, dear," my mother states.

"Look, he's two years younger than Cathy, and she's thirty-seven," my father argues.

"Well, if anyone should remember how old he is it would certainly be me. I could never forget that delivery." It is the end of the dispute. My mother always wins this kind of argument.

"Mommy, we only have twenty-six."

"You're thirty-eight?" Sam asks. It is loneliness that steals years, more than fear.

"It will have to do, sweetie." I line the candles up in a row. At quarter to eleven, the children are back, looking for food like beggars, stretching their hands across the table. They make fingerprint clouds on the glass, casting the map into shadow. Dollops of spilled marmalade and jam catch the sun's rays and glow. Tegan licks the blue edge of the table and tastes strawberry. She opens her palm and drops small toys onto a plate: a pink doll's comb with some teeth missing; a Lego star fighter with one yellow arm; broken crayons peeled of their paper wrappers, round and smooth like beads, their wax softened by a child's warm hand.

Sam stares at his youngest daughter's assorted collection, and then pushes away from the table. He moves towards the coffee maker but changes his mind and floats into the living room with an empty cup. The north-facing window at the far end is ablaze with colour. Burnt orange leaves from the mountain ash are brushing against the glass. I watch my husband stand before the tree, fingers on the windowpane. Is he remembering or imagining—the small red berries, hanging like miniature grapes—the colour of a wound or the shade of a woman's lips? Does he taste copper in the soft metal of his tongue? Sam brings his hand to his throat. Fingers caress the thin scar like it's a necklace. Is there something caught under the skin? Not a tumour. The lump was cut out eight months ago, so that can't be right. It must be the choking hold of a truth or fear. An overseas call will never come? A sailor his wife once loved? Or is his future slipping away by a migrant cancer cell?

Somewhere the slow melting of bones and skin has begun. And love.

Icarus is falling.

DURING THE LAST EIGHT years, my brother has lived life like it's a bold adventure. Sometimes I forget there was a time when he had no ambition at all.

"Gotta get out of here, little brother."

"No kidding," he agrees.

Springsteen's voice calls to the masses from three-foot speakers. I lean against David's mattress and stare at the posters on the wall—a sketch of the Olympic Stadium in Montreal, a sailboat flying a spinnaker.

"Really, David. It's time to move out. You're twenty-four. You are living in your childhood bedroom. And it has orange carpet!"

"Yeah," he says, nodding slowly while taking *Led Zeppelin II* out of its sleeve. "Not sure what orange carpet has to do with it...."

"Well, it's cold to sit on, for one thing, but what I mean is, what are you going to do with your life?"

"What are *you* going to do?" he fires back, and then softens his tone. "What about this sailor? Are you going back?"

"I don't think so. I just can't see that life for me."

"So what's next?"

Now it's my turn to shrug. I flip through a stack of coloured albums, and try to look interested. *Running on Empty. Midnight Lightning.* We avoid the hard questions with his music.

A week later I return to Toronto and Sam. We book round-the-world airline tickets with eight stops spread out over a year. Travelling quells the confusion about what to do with a life.

You should try it, I write to David from Thailand. *Get out of the basement and see the world.*

My father leaves the table.

He opens the back door and goes out to the yard. He is wearing blue mechanic's coveralls, the pair he's worked in for forty years. There are streaks of paint on the left shoulder where he leaned on a wall. The fingerprints on his thighs are like little comets from the year the colour "Harvest Gold" appeared on the house siding.

My love of sweeping must come from my father. He slams the wide broom against the deck. Each thud is followed by a swish of nylon bristles. The pinecones flutter and bounce away. He attacks until the cones are corralled and then scoops them with his bare hands into the garbage bag. It is a never-ending battle—eighty-year-old fir trees recklessly trying to seed themselves. Over my father's head, a gust of wind is caught in the trees. Boughs rise and fall discordantly. More cones rattle down on the deck. He stops sweeping and lifts his shoulders, sighing at the futility.

Two years before David is born, my father maps body and airplane parts on a prairie field. He is part of an air force team sent out to investigate why a plane crashed on a clear night.

My father thinks the night can fool a navigator. Northern lights twist the sky onto its side, waves of pink and green break like surf. *I don't know where we are,* says a voice. (Find the horizon.) The moon is a white marble rolling over the black edge of night. *We're going the wrong way.* (Find Orion.) The stars are wet flickers of dust. *We're upside-down.* (Find land, son.)

My father loves in muted ways.

"Can we have the black cookies now, Mommy? You promised."

Is it noon already?

Three brown-eyed children lean against the backs of chairs, tucking their knees under small chins. They twist the chocolate tops and lick the white icing with insect tongues. Their legs open and close like butterfly wings.

Silent words rise and fall. The secret tightens under my ribs.

MY ELDEST DAUGHTER PLACES a finger in the centre of a red ribbon and allows her uncle to tighten a knot.

"I'm stuck," Victoria squeals, wriggling her hand now joined to a length of dowel.

"Then you'll have to fly up too," David teases her. "Because I'm not going to abandon the one and only kite I've ever made just because you won't let go."

She laughs at his eyes. The wind flutters her jacket.

They walk to the park connected by paper, wood, ribbon, and a large hand with a smaller palm tucked inside. Above their heads, the afternoon sky waits to be stamped by a white kite with a flying tail of red bows. On a low rise of earth at one end of the field they place their backs to the wind. David licks his finger and holds it in the air.

"It's coming from the east," he says. "Not a good sign, but it could change. Winds are very capricious."

Victoria smiles at the word and the shape of his lips because it looks like he's kissing the air.

"I think we're ready for the big pond," David says to me over the phone on a July evening. He's calling from Fionnphort on the Scottish Isle of Mull. "We'll leave here next month. Azores first, then Madeira. That gives us lots of time to get out of the North Atlantic before the autumn equinox storms come."

"How long will it take you?" I ask.

"Two weeks, I think." His voice drops. Sounds serious. That's good, I think. He won't do anything stupid. The phone line crackles, reminding me of how far away he is. "We'll see how it all turns out, Cath."

"Say bye to Sarah for me," I tell him.

"We'll call as soon as we reach land."

My lungs draw in as I remember this promise.

He knew what he was getting into, I tell myself. He wasn't too bold, not over-confident. He wasn't cocky. Just brave.

For years, David has sought freedom from modern North American definitions of a successful life. He made a choice that he thought was available to all of us—to allow the imagination to be bigger than the body.

I DRAG MY LITTLE brother down the hill and across the field behind our elementary school. Overhead, a plane roars on take-off. David jumps and claws at the air as if an invisible ladder is trailing behind the red-striped tail.

"It's a *Voodoo!*" he shouts.

We watch the fighter jet climb quickly, its sleek body slicing through the clouds like a steel knife. The rumble from its engines lingers in the air long after the plane has disappeared. Our skin prickles with the sound.

"It's gone, David," I say, tugging at his hand. "Let's go."

He follows me but checks the sky with upturned glances.

We find the nest hidden in a clump of dry stalks—four pink mouths retching at the air. These are the baby meadowlarks everyone was talking about after recess. David and I lie down on our stomachs, stretching across the yellowed grass, our heads touching. We are thrilled by the discovery of these wild lives, here in the ordered world of air force houses and uniformed fathers.

The birds are fascinating at first, and maybe a little sweet in their smallness, but after a few minutes they appear malformed and desperate. Deep throats eclipse their thin bodies. Peeping and peeping without stop, we stare at their panic. Gaping-mouthed fear.

"Let's feed them," David says, as he pulls at tufts of grass.

I don't answer him. The darkness that extends into the birds' twisting bodies has caught hold of me. My chest is pressing into the earth like a weight has been dropped onto my back. How are these birds going to survive? They're too exposed. Children play here. Bikes roll down the hill. Why did the mother choose this place?

"We need worms," David whispers. His hands jam into the dirt.

I think about lifting the nest and carrying it, but to where? Where are wild creatures safe?

"Help me dig," he says.

His fingers search in the crumbling earth, the fingernails edged in black. Confused by my feeling of hopelessness, my hands remain still.

The clock shows ten after one.

"I'll start the cake now," my mother says and she pours a Duncan Hines mix into a bowl, spilling grey flour onto the counter. David would have made the cake from scratch and used a wooden spoon to beat it. She pries open a blue styrofoam carton and takes out two eggs.

"Do you still have the juggling balls?" I ask.

"Oh yes," she laughs. "They're in the fridge at home."

"WANT AN EGG, DAVID?" I ask. I open my parents' fridge and remove one from the egg holder.

"Sure."

"Catch." I toss it high into the air. "Or would you like two?"

"What the hell?" he shouts, swinging his hands over his head, grappling for the falling white orbs. "Are you nuts?"

Before I can ask if he'd like three, perhaps scrambled, the first egg-shaped rubber ball bounces on the kitchen table and the second off his head.

"Merry Christmas, David!"

My mother and I laugh until tears spill down our cheeks, into our mouths.

After breakfast, I teach him how to juggle in my parent's low-ceilinged living room. His skill surpasses mine quickly. The clown in David finds the rhythm, the humour, and the magic of keeping things afloat. Unlike me, he doesn't need Thai mushrooms to keep the balls moving slowly through air like a time-exposure photograph of waxing moons.

For the next six months, he and my mother have a game they never tire of. They toss rubber eggs at any poor soul who comes through the back door.

"You know Cathy, I'm glad your travelling days are over," my mother says while scraping the chocolate batter into a pan lined with waxed paper. "Now that you're married and have children, I don't have to worry about you. If David would just come home, I could relax."

The children are back in the kitchen asking for more food. I give them beaters and a wooden spoon and then make Kraft dinner. They swallow the rubbery tubes whole. Their tongues are the colour of mashed cheezies.

"Mommy?"

"Yes?"

"If Uncle David died, would I die too?" I look down at the table. Toast bones, apple cores, shrivelled bacon. I hold my breath to quiet the rattle under my ribs. I cannot bear to see my mother's face.

"Why would you die, sweetie?"

David, his mouth returned to pink, whispers, "Because we have the same name, Mommy."

I am holding my brother's life in the soft flesh of my throat. I dare not tell for fear I'll drop the ball of thread and lose us. If I speak, will the sky fall in? I am sister, daughter, wife, and mother—there is no myth to guide me with this question. What will ease the weight of all those incarnations?

MOMENTS IN MY LIFE are frozen, permanent photographs.

My parents and siblings are wedged inside a red Bombardier crawling over the Columbia Icefield. We look down into crevasses and fissures where the glacier has split and yawned to alarming-sized gaps. It's like staring down the side of a frozen wave, forty feet deep. The ice is the colour of a sapphire and dense as stone.

I imagine myself slipping into that allurement of blue. It is bright under the ice, not the darkness one would expect but a silvery light—trapped ancient sunrays, pressed out of time. I hear the call of the sea, echoing like a shell held close to my ear. If I descend even further there will be caverns large as cathedrals, and the tunnels and pathways of a hidden labyrinth unknown to the living. Ice as secretive as an ocean.

I can still see them, my mother's hand grasping David's collar as he leans over the deep chasm. She holds him, he lets his body fall forward. He is not afraid his mother will let go. His face glows in the light.

At half-past two, the milk in the coffee is floating in white lumps. My mother slips quietly from the table, a crumb-filled napkin slides from her lap to the floor. I can hear the washing machine in the basement filling with water, then the muffled sound of clothes being pushed under the suds. A cotton shirt floats up. The corner of a collar breaking through the spume. A red sail. She pushes the shirt to the bottom and drops the metal lid loudly. Soapsuds circle her elbow. The machine agitates against her belly.

Birthdays always do this to her, remind her of the days when her babies were turned, tugged, pushed, finally spilling out of the river that began in her. She has memories she won't abandon—the fuming last baby she was presented with, the years of anemia and depression that weighed her down while she scrubbed children and waxed floors. Those were the blue years in the fight for order. My mother once told me, "A good day was when I was the first one on the street to have my laundry on the line."

"YOU'RE NOT THE WOMAN you used to be," David says. His words descend like a curse. I am on my hands and knees wiping spilled apple juice. Six-month-old Tegan cries in another room. My brother keeps flipping through a yachting magazine at the kitchen table. I look up at him and see the wind in his eyes.

Is he criticizing, pitying, or challenging me—as well as being insensitive? Is it only Desire he understands?

Yes, Love, Demeter's soft breast, has changed me. There are rhythms in my life now, and responsibilities that must be met. I rinse the rag in the old porcelain sink and return to my knees, sliding the cloth across the floor with wide strokes. The sea-green linoleum turns dark. My shoulders sink as if I'm falling. Am I cowering under Regret and Duty, those minor goddesses living in the broom closet that David has just set free?

I sailed to Turkey naked once. I wish I had asked him: How are we certain which longings in our bodies are the true ones?

I am the only one left at the table at 4 o'clock. I write the word *AND* with the birthday candles. My mother passes by me, her arms filled with warm laundry. Panties in halves. Sheets folded like flags. Palm-smoothed t-shirts with arms tucked under like well-behaved children. "Maybe he phoned Diane, when he couldn't reach us at home," she comments on her way upstairs. My older sister in Winnipeg doesn't approve of David's lifestyle but she'll accept a collect call. She likes to talk to him.

A trail of warm air follows after my mother, caressing my face gently. But it is the sharp scent of detergent that lingers, the sting of lemon.

I hear the washing machine empty its suds in a furious rush. I scratch at the yolk-stained table. Throughout history, women have made an art of waiting for men to return from sea or war or some other adventure. The women silently weave the heroic tales, then unravel their work and begin again, perhaps telling the story a little differently each time, perhaps imagining if it was their own.

ON THEIR FIRST DATE, David and Sarah go down to the Tasman Sea. On a high sandstone cliff, hanging over the beach, a pattern of coarse lace is carved into the rock.

"It's like a honeycomb," my brother says.

"Salt and sand create that effect," Sarah explains. She whips her towel into the breeze. "When the wind blasts against the cliff face, crystallizing salt helps to force the sand grains out. It leaves little connected hollows. You're right. Just like a honeycomb." Sarah spreads the towel on the sand, removing a few rocks from underneath. She weighs them in her hand. "I studied geology."

David watches her slip out of her shorts, pull her t-shirt over the short-cropped hair and lie on her stomach with her feet pointing towards the ripple of waves. She pushes her hips and breasts down until she has carved the sand to suit her shape. David imagines what it would be like to be the shore under her. A prairie wind scrapes at the spaces between his vertebrae. He reaches out for the dark V of hair at her neck, traces the spine's row of bones, and hesitates at the damp valley of her lower back.

His soul rolls.

Saliva pools under his tongue and wets the corner of his mouth.

Islands and seas and tears will rise into being from his first words of love to Sarah. Perhaps he says, "You're a little red. Would you like some sunscreen?" Or, as he rubs lotion over her body with calloused fingertips: "I've never oiled an English back before." But I think he says (my brother who loves sea stories), "I see the curling crests of an ocean tumbling on your back. There is a woman clinging to the back of a white bull as he plows through the waves. Her hand holds one of the long horns. For balance. I am uncertain if she is willing or not."

"Why is the bull with the woman?" Sarah asks.

"Because somewhere it is written that he should be."

David loosens the knot at the back of her bathing suit and sees it for the first time. The only thing in the world—a narrow white band, not as wide as his finger, of untanned skin belonging to a woman. He draws his oily finger along her back to where her left breast starts to curve. The stripe darkens like a wet stone. "You have a horizon line," he says. "It separates the sea from the sky." He envisions making his body thin enough to lie down in it.

Sarah asks, "Why do you think the woman is with the bull?"

For a thousand years he falls towards the white line, the image of his desire burning across his eyes. As he plummets he wonders about her question. Is it the bull's lust that secures the woman to his back? Is it fear of the sea that keeps her thighs pressed tight to his flank? What is the true nature of the woman's desire?

Just before he falls into her, floating above the sea scent of skin, I want my brother to understand that Love is improbable and women know this. I want him to realize that the woman's story is unfinished.

David says to Sarah, "She's hanging on to see what will happen next."

They couldn't say, why him, why her, why that moment in time on the edge of a sea, love entered the world from the knot of their bodies. They filled, expanded, and shaped each other.

David had written that *Mugwump* was only twenty-seven feet in length but her small cabin felt spacious. The hull seemed to stretch to make room for them. They liked to lie together on the salon bench waiting for the kettle to boil. A room of rising steam, dampened walls, the sweet scent of teak oil. Perhaps this feeling of space made them think the ocean was smaller than it was.

THE DAY HAS ENDED with no call. I climb into bed with my son, smell the cinnamon hair at his neck, curl his jelly-like body into mine. I rub his back, patting at the green pajamas with the little white raised turtles. I try to imagine this body so far from my own. To protect this son is the will of my limbs and yet someday he will not be saved, will not need to be saved by me, and then what? What of the shell of the woman when love casts it off? We close our arms around what we must love and find it gone, missing from our shores.

Is the full weight of love despair?

I wake from a dream, my face wet. I am swimming in blue. There is no beginning or end to blue, no horizon line to separate the dream from my waking. I raise my arm and translucent sails cling to my skin like mouths to a nipple. A flotilla of jellyfish surrounds me. From a far-off shore, a stone skips across the water. There are circles in the blue. The sailors-by-the-wind catch the breeze and are gone.

What is the beginning of this story?

She says yes. She whispers yes, dreams of yes, nods yes. Her breasts rise with yes, she sighs with yes, spreads her legs apart with yes, opens her throat with yes, writes yes on his skin with her fingertips, says yes with her eyes and her furrowed brow, arches her back with yes, smiles, oh, she smiles her yes and he thinks he has conquered her—the dream coming alive under his tongue. Yet he knows it isn't him any longer, isn't his skin or his mouth or his body. It is the world, the beginning working through him, the birthing of the old dream, and he breathes out, knowing for the first time what grace is.

SOMEWHERE IN THE MIDDLE
OF THE ATLANTIC

Life is a daring adventure or
nothing at all.

HELEN KELLER

OCTOBER 1. *This is what I do when you don't call from an island somewhere in the middle of the Atlantic:*

I finally find what I am looking for in a pile of unopened junk mail—David's postcard from Ireland. The photograph is an aerial shot of the Black Fort on Inishmore, one of the Aran Islands on the west coast. Dark stone walls cut across a rocky promontory surrounded by water on three sides. The cliffs are hundreds of feet high, angled and cantilevered over the sea. Pieces of the island must have broken away over time. If the world had an edge to fall from, here it is.

Hi!
Well, it's not the Azores yet! We had a bit of a setback when our
engine quit off the Irish Coast. We need it to charge the batteries.
We put in to Broad Haven and anchored, expecting to stop for a
few hours while I fixed it. It was a week before we set off again!
Sitting out two days of gales but it's fixed at last. We had a fast
run down to Castletown for reprovisioning. We've left it a little
late for the Azores so tomorrow we set off for Madeira!
Love Uncle Dave

I carry an atlas into the bedroom and lock the door.
Flipping pages against my thumb, I find Ireland. My eye wan-
ders over the country with a moment of pleasure. *Limerick.*
Tipperary. Ireland is a poem—every mile named with rhythmic
compound phrases. I follow the coastlines where the Irish
Gaelic words float like piers jutting into the sea. From the bay
of Broadhaven I trace my finger south: Achill Head, Kilkieran
Bay, Aran Islands, Skellig Rocks, Dursey Head, and finally
Castletownbere in Bantry Bay. This must be the place David is
referring to in the postcard. Two peninsulas further is Mizen
Head and then the most southerly point of Ireland, Fastnet
Rock. I know this name. The Rock is the rounding point in
the famous Cowes to Portsmouth yacht race. In 1979, a freak
storm turned the Fastnet Race into a tragedy: dozens of boats
abandoned, some sunk, a hundred sailors rescued and fifteen
dead. Every British sailor knows this story. Simon had told it
to me after we had crossed to the island of Naxos.

I turn to the front of the atlas for a map of Europe. The
borders of the countries are thick and brightly coloured like a
child's school map. I look along the coastlines of France, Spain,
and Portugal but I cannot find the Azores or Madeira. They are
too far off the European shores. A map of northwestern Africa

reveals Madeira's location—due west of Casablanca, five hundred miles from the coast of Morocco. On the same page, the Azores can be seen in the top left-hand corner, nine islands floating alone in an ocean-blue box without context to any continent. I leaf through more maps but I can't find one that shows where the Portuguese archipelago emerges out of the Atlantic. The western hemisphere as a whole seems to be missing from the book.

I go down to the kitchen and find Mom playing a game of solitaire. Fingerprints have re-emerged along the thick blue edges of the table. I polished the surface after dinner, lightly warning everyone not to touch the surface, but it can't be helped. Skin always leaves marks. Not just fingers. Entire palms. Reversed maps of fate. And elbows, the driest skin on our bodies, press circles while holding the weight of a head.

"Where's Dad?" I ask.

"He's bottling wine with Sam."

I lean down the basement stairwell and smell fermenting grape juice. Deep male voices echo off the concrete walls. There's a laugh, followed by a muffled, "Shit." Another laugh. I can hear the groan of the bottling arm pushing corks into glass necks.

I keep a globe on a desk in the far corner of the kitchen. New countries with altered borders have emerged since I bought it seventeen years ago, but the oceans and islands are in the same place. I try to look casual as I carry the dented world like a handbag up the stairs. Crossing the threshold of my bedroom, I hear Mom snapping cards.

I easily find the slightly raised ridge of the Rocky Mountains—landlocked *CALGARY* is typed over a summit. My fingertips follow the serpentine relief, no wider than a series of swollen mosquito bites, extending north to Alaska and south to Argentina's heel—a range the length of the earth.

It would be easy to miss the Azores on a globe if you weren't looking for them. The dotted blue lines indicating sea currents swirl clockwise around the Atlantic basin, almost obscuring the names of the islands. I can make out São Jorge, Faial, Pico, São Miguel. I am surprised to see that the islands lie almost equidistant between Newfoundland and Portugal, eight hundred miles from each shore. Why are they even here? Volcanic activity? What else thrusts peaks of land out of the middle of the ocean? I can understand why David and Sarah decided to give them a miss. The islands are far off their course.

The island of Madeira lies southeast from the Azores. Taking the gold chain from around my neck, I measure the distance between Ireland and Madeira—twenty degrees of latitude, 1,200 miles, like travelling from Toronto to the Arctic Circle. Suddenly, my brother's voyage seems to be a defiant act of will. An immense expanse of sea needs to be crossed with no opportunities for rest.

What was he thinking?

And what was I thinking?

In the last month I have held little of my brother in my mind. How carelessly I slipped into neglectfulness, and now I find myself in the present with nothing but questions. I am ashamed. One of the acts of love is to hold memory.

I pick up the postcard again and study it closely. A hundred words penned in a shaky scrawl. David's handwriting always has the look of nervousness, a corporeal energy that must be harnessed and focused to complete the loops of letters and squeeze his thoughts into available space. His sentences are casual but the exclamation marks flash excitement. *Well, it's not the Azores yet!* And the word *tomorrow* feels hopeful and promising. I flip the postcard back and forth and then hold it to my forehead, searching my memory. The cancel date on the stamp is too faint to read and I can't remember when the card arrived. Two weeks ago, three weeks, four?

OCTOBER 9. *This is what happens when I insist on keeping the secret that you are sailing somewhere in the middle of the Atlantic:*

"You should have told them," says Sam.

We watch the car pull away. Mom's palm is pressed against the window.

"Next year, we'll come to you!" I shout.

The children race the car down to the next block, swinging their arms in exuberant gestures of goodbye. Dad keeps pace with them.

"I just couldn't, Sam."

"You're going to have to tell them soon."

"Maybe not. David and Sarah are a little behind schedule. That can't be unusual. Maybe they're en route to the Canary Islands now and they'll call from there."

"Let's hope so." Sam turns and walks into the house.

David should have to tell our parents where he is, not me, I think sulkily. It was his idea to keep this voyage a secret. I sit down on the curb and look to the park on the other side of the street. The road seems to have stretched, widened into a dark, grey river that can't be crossed.

When there is no call from David on his birthday and no calls on the days following, no one says a thing. The ritual has been observed and put away for another year. Leftover cake is consumed, the crumbs wiped and the table made tidy. Only a deck of cards remains. My parents and I wade privately with our unspoken thoughts. Dad stares out windows with his fingertips on the glass, a spectral form—unlike him to stand so still. Mom pulls the curled dead leaves from my houseplants. We move around each other, the gestures of our hands carrying life forward—combing the children's hair, stirring milk into coffee, tugging at the laces of shoes. They don't ask me any questions that make it difficult to avoid the truth, like: *Do you know where David and Sarah are?* or *What did he tell you about their plans?* (Would I have lied outright? Or deflected with swift talk?) I offer them nothing.

The strained silence in the household is punctured when Mom and I fight about the Thanksgiving turkey. She pronounces angrily that there is no way that bird is going to fit into my new, somewhat smaller, convection oven. I claim it will. My punishment for being right is I have to truss the turkey myself while she gives tight-lipped instructions over my shoulder. Plans are changed to return to Winnipeg early.

In the morning, David helps his grandfather wash the car. His small hand drags a sopping rag across the bumper. Soap bubbles drip to the asphalt.

"We should really head home. I've still got a lot of work to do before winter comes," Dad offers as an explanation while he polishes the hubcaps. I picture the backyard of my childhood home. The grass should be mowed one last time before the first snowfall. Lawn furniture needs to be dragged back into the garage. The garden beds must be mulched with dried leaves.

I go back into the house and return with a box filled with Ritz crackers and cheese and a carafe of coffee.

Mom and I hug goodbye on the sidewalk. Yellow leaves swirl around our feet, the debris of autumn sweeping by. I let my mother and father go without telling them anything and now I wonder what this secret will do—the unspoken worry for their son, a shadow following them home, eight hundred miles of shorn prairie, the harvest over.

OCTOBER 10. *This is what Sam thinks while you are somewhere in the middle of the Atlantic:*

"I have no idea," Sam answers when I ask him if he remembers what date David and Sarah were supposed to leave Ireland. He turns back to the contents of his sock drawer. He is trying to make a pair so he can finish dressing and get to the cancer clinic for his first nuclear medicine scan since the surgery.

"I am going to phone Sarah's mother tomorrow," I say. "Maybe she's heard something."

"I hope so. It was a reckless thing to do."

Reckless. The word feels like a blow to my chest.

"You really think so?"

"I just think they didn't have enough experience to have tried this kind of trip. Think about it. The boat's small. What? Under thirty feet? And there's only two of them." On the top of the dresser a row of single socks lengthens in a weird game of sock solitaire.

"Well, I guess they thought they were ready. What else was there to do?"

"They could have crewed on another boat," he says, a hand reaching into the drawer. "Got some experience doing ocean crossings first." Sam is right but I'm suddenly angry. He's picked the wrong moment to give his opinion. And, yes, crewing would have been prudent but David isn't that patient. He believed he could do this as well as anyone else.

"Here, these socks are close enough," I say, handing him two strays. I sweep the rest back into the drawer and push it roughly. The slides scrape against the worn grooves—the wood shaving into dust. Sam has done his share of dumb things and has the scars to show it. I bite my tongue, though I want to remind him of times when I thought he had been rash, or disregarded danger, particularly his avoidance of the ear, nose, and throat specialist for five years.

On a cold January day, I am ushered into in a pale green hospital room.

"The tumour on the thyroid was as big as a man's fist," the young-looking, female surgeon explains to me. "It was malignant so we took everything out." Her eyes leave my face, glancing briefly towards the window and the scattering of snowflakes hanging in air. The word *malignant* floats like a balloon between us. "I believe I got it all," she assures, her voice deepening. When I nod that I understand, she continues. "Another problem has presented itself. There's some internal bleeding. I have to open up your husband again."

I can see the edge of the scalpel slicing open the flooding throat. Blood spills over a gowned shoulder onto polished linoleum floors.

My skin turns cold. My limbs sink like iron filings are shuffling through the veins. A spasm of fear tears at my muscles as the darkness crosses a threshold.

Something is slipping away—our safe and perfect lives.

At the Tom Baker Cancer Clinic, the technician tells Sam to lie down on the narrow table and then he leaves. We are alone in the chapel-dim room. The machine slowly rolls over Sam like a priest's blessing, its hushed movement silencing us. This cancer fell like a warning, a small voice reminding us that there is something we have forgotten, something we were supposed to do with our lives.

Don't waste them, the machine hums.

As the scanner travels up Sam's body, a blue computer screen records the imaging. Small white stars appear, hinting at the shape of a man. There is a cluster of light in the abdomen but in the throat area, where an enlarged thyroid once reduced the trachea by half, only a black hole remains. I look down at Sam. His body seems to be floating upward as if it might hit the flat panel above him. I should do something, I think, or say something that will keep him on the table. I reach out but my hand is floating too, unattached to my arm. I am separating into pieces, the mind outside the body watching the wreckage. When the machine stops, Sam turns his head to look at the screen. "It doesn't look good, does it?"

"We don't know what we're looking at," I answer. It's not a real body, I tell myself. It's a constellation. A galaxy of fear exploding across the screen.

When the technician returns, he turns on the lights. The fluorescents flicker. "I'll be back in a few minutes—I just have to analyze the image." I blink like I am waking up. Sam and I look away as if we've seen each other's nightmare. The chilled flesh.

"All clear," the technician says as he flings the door open.

"What about those stars on the screen?" I ask him.

"Stars? Oh, the imaging? That's the remainder of the radioactive iodine. It's concentrated in the gut because it hasn't completely broken down yet. There's nothing there. The cancer's gone. Go buy a lottery ticket."

We leave the room, walk down the halls, and ride up the elevator. The reception area doors open into sunlight. I feel like we're teenagers defiantly walking out of school in the middle of the day and no one is bothering to stop us.

Somehow, we've gotten away with it. When we get to the parking lot neither one of us can remember where we put the truck. We wander up and down the rows.

"The truck is maroon-coloured, right?" asks Sam.

It will be all right, I repeat over and over. Sam won't die. My children will have a father.

"Let's have a party tonight. At Minos's. I feel like breaking a plate."

From the car, I telephone to make a dinner reservation for twenty, no, thirty. When I'm put on hold, I keep the phone pressed tight to my ear, waiting for the voice to return.

OCTOBER 11. *This is what I say to Sarah's mother who knows you are somewhere in the middle of the Atlantic:*

"Is it raining?" I ask.

"Oh, yes," says Heather, drawing out the word *yes* so it rings like a musical note. "Autumn is very wet on Mull. I can't see out of the windows." I remember the Scottish-style white-washed house and the sheep's pasture that slopes down to the only road leading to Fionnphort. "Our summer was very good though," Heather continues. "Lots of sun."

"I remember Mull as mostly having blue skies."

"We did have a nice spring that year," she says. "You're calling about Dave, now, aren't you?"

"I haven't heard from him, Heather. They must be there by now." I hold my breath, feel my thoat contract.

"We haven't heard a thing, either," she sighs. "The coast-guard in Falmouth, England has been contacted and made aware of the situation." There is a *situation,* now. I reach for the teapot and a cup.

"When did they leave?" I ask.

"They had some problems with the boat in Ireland so they left later than they wanted to. Sarah called on August thirtieth from Castletownbere saying they were leaving for Madeira the next day."

Five weeks ago.

"We think it should have taken them about ten days or perhaps fourteen or even longer. Could be longer," Heather says.

Ten. Fourteen. Longer.

I add up the numbers in my head—*Mugwump* is forty days gone. I stir milk into a cup of amber-coloured tea. A small depression, the size of a thumbprint, falls in the centre like a whirlpool.

"How long has the coastguard known?" I ask.

"A few days now."

Shit, why didn't she call earlier? I should have called her.

"You must be very worried, Heather."

Why were we not calling?

"Well, yes, of course, we are concerned, but now that the coastguard is aware of the situation we are hopeful it will turn out all right." Her voice has become lighter in tone but louder. I realize I shouldn't have said that. *Very worried.* She's Sarah's *mother.*

"I have absolute faith in your brother, Cathy," Heather assures me.

What is there to say to that? *I'm glad you feel that way? Because I'm feeling quite sick that my brother may have dragged your daughter off into the ocean and now she's missing.* I know there was no dragging of Sarah, but still, this all began as David's dream.

OCTOBER 12. *This is what the North Atlantic Maritime Rescue Coordination Centre in Falmouth, England, tells me while* Mugwump *is somewhere in the middle of the Atlantic:*

"There of course will be no physical search." The voice on the end of the line has a crisp British accent. "The size of the area is five million square kilometers. And we have no idea where they might be."

"Of course," I agree readily. *Of course?* Of course. It's a huge fucking ocean.

"And you must remember, Miss, that there have been no radio distress calls. None whatsoever."

"But that could mean they don't have a working radio."

"Yes, it could mean that."

"So, what will you do?"

"We have notified all Western European Rescue Operations. A request has been made for the Spanish, French, and Portuguese harbours to check their records to see if *Mugwump* has put into port anywhere. We have made one Inmarsat broadcast to ships on the North Atlantic, and another radio broadcast will be extended to include the Canaries and Gibraltar. Casablanca and New York have also been notified. Transatlantic airlines as well."

"So everyone knows?" I ask.

"We just broadcast the information."

"Can I ask you something?"

"Yes."

"How long do you think it should have taken them to get to Madeira from Ireland?"

"Well, there are many factors to consider. Wind. Keel. Size of sails. Strength of the crew. But I think about ten days to two weeks—basically what your brother thought."

"Have there been any storms in the area that might have caused problems?" I ask.

"Yes, there have been storms. Storms are normal for this time of year. But there have been no boats reported damaged or missing because of them."

Normal is good, I think. Normal is manageable.

"What else can you tell me about *Mugwump*?" I am asked.

"Like what?"

"Significant colours or markings on the sails and hull. Types of radios on board, call signals, planned radio contact with shore stations. A life raft description would be very helpful or any information about navigational tools, GPS, and EPIRB."

"I'm afraid I don't know anything."

"Well, see what you can find out. There's someone here twenty-four hours a day. And of course we'll call you if we hear anything. Now, can you tell me something about your brother and Sarah?"

OCTOBER 13. *This is how I remember Sarah who is with you somewhere in the middle of the Atlantic:*

Sarah moves like a cat, linked to the earth.

She is lithe. Her movements are timed, considered, and purposeful. Unlike David she does not have a personality that shows itself through expansive physical motion, it is more like her limbs and mind move as one—a unity of muscle and thought. If you call her from across a room she will turn her head and body with the same motion. When asked a question, Sarah takes her time formulating an answer, and when she speaks, her body has a faint vibration like her skin is answering as well.

Sarah is pretty. Slim. About five-and-a-half feet. Her eyes are blue. Her brown hair is hennaed into the colours of a sunset.

I catch a glimpse of the hair dying ritual when I pass by my basement bathroom on the way to the laundry room. Sarah is sitting on the closed lid of the toilet while David is snapping rubber gloves over his hands like a surgeon. Taking a thin black comb, he draws the teeth across her scalp from back to front. The parted hair reveals a strip of pale flesh. With a brush he paints the row with the brown paste. Sarah puts her hands on his hips.

I move past them, lowering my eyes, a basket overflowing with tiny shirts and baby sleepers tucked under my arm.

OCTOBER 14. *This is what your older brother says while you are somewhere in the middle of the Atlantic:*

"David's missing," I say into the phone.

"What do you mean, missing?" Kerry asks.

"David and Sarah left Ireland in their boat on August thirty-first. No one's heard from them for over a month."

"What? Where were they going?" His mouth is pressed close to the receiver.

"Madeira."

"I don't think I even know where that is."

"It's off the coast of Africa. He didn't tell anyone because he thought he'd get all kinds of flak for it."

"Well, he was right about that. So, what else do you know?"

"Sarah's mom called the British Coastguard over a week ago. Two offshore radio broadcasts have been made but no yachts or ships have responded with any information about *Mugwump*. The coastguard has checked with coastal authorities but there's no record of the yacht in any European port. I've also made some calls. Three European coastguards, two Canadian Consulates, and the Department of External Affairs. No one knows anything." My chest seizes as the details spill out. I tell him everything I know but not what I've imagined.

"You've done a good job, Cath," he offers gently. He doesn't ask why I didn't call him sooner. He never suggests that I should have started asking questions in the middle of September instead of a month later.

"What else should we do, Kerry?"

"Let me think." The phone is silent for a moment. I hear him writing something down, a pencil scratching on paper. I look out the window to the park across the street. I imagine how my home province of Manitoba will look next month—a thin layer of early snow covering the roads and fields, pale footprints in long straight lines, and a thousand grey lakes turned wild by November winds.

My brothers launch a sixteen-foot sailboat into the waters of Lake Winnipeg. The boat belongs to Kerry but it is his younger brother who is teaching him to sail. They navigate the wooden craft, staying in sight of land, never trying to cross the huge prairie lake with its choppy waves and changing winds. According to Kerry, David is a decent sailor, quick and responsive, but a poor teacher who grows impatient with Kerry's slow tacking. On the water, the two brothers often argue.

On an August morning, David sets off in the boat without his older brother's permission. The wind is strong and David plans to raise all the sails and have a brisk ride before Kerry knows he's gone. But, not far from shore, the wind changes direction suddenly, grabs at the main, and forces the boat onto its side. The mast breaks in two.

I hear about the accident when my angry brothers walk in the house with the torn sail.

"Can you fix it, Cathy?" Kerry asks.

It's a six-foot tear in the middle of the triangle. I stuff the canvas under my Singer sewing machine. There is so much material I have to hold the sail down with my chin so I can see the stitching line. It takes me hours to fix what the wind and the water had done in seconds.

"Was there any radio contact after David and Sarah left Ireland?" Kerry asks.

"Just once. They contacted the Valencia Island Coastguard when they were southwest of Mizen Head."

"Do you know if they had an EPIRB?"

"Heather said they had one, but the coastguard is doubtful. Normally, yachts register EPIRBs with coastguard stations and they have no record of one for *Mugwump*."

"They should have had one," Kerry sighs. "With this kind of satellite technology available now it's stupid not to. They vastly improve the chances of being rescued."

"David probably thought that if something went wrong, who'd be close enough to save them anyway? Like sailors who never learn how to swim. And besides, they're probably expensive." David and Sarah had had just enough money to buy *Mugwump* and outfit her. Because they planned to sail all the way to the Caribbean before seeking work as a day charter, they would have weighed the pros and cons of spending money on the locating device.

"Mom and Dad would have bought them one." Kerry's voice is fading.

He sounds cold, like a shiver has lifted skin away from muscle.

"Should I tell them?" My stomach lurches.

"Let's wait a bit longer, a couple of days. Maybe there'll be some news. I'm going to make some calls and try the Internet."

More waiting. Each hour, each day, is a battle between longing and dread. I see my two brothers pulling the never-named blue hull out of the water. There are whitecaps. David is insisting it was a perfect day for a sail.

"Do you remember when David dumped your boat?" I ask.

"Yeah," he says, softly. "It was such a dumb thing to do. The winds were gusting like crazy."

OCTOBER 15. *This is what I imagine at night while the wind is hammering at the windows and you are somewhere in the middle of the Atlantic:*

A torn sail snaps like a standard in war.

A mast is ripped from the deck and falls, a plunging sword driving through shadows to the deep.

An overturned keel slices the water like the dorsal fin of a killer whale.

The sea is black. Not a flickering star in the waves.

OCTOBER 16. *This is how an optimistic coastguard talks while you are somewhere in the middle of the Atlantic:*

"No news is good news," says the coastguard, his tone cheery even though it is evening in England. In three days I've talked to four different men. I wonder if they hold up the phone mouthing, *Whose turn is it to talk to the woman from Canada?*

"Is that like 'hope for the best, prepare for the worst'?" I ask, meeting his cliché with another.

"Oh, no, Miss, I really mean this. In this case, no news *is* good news," he insists. "There have been no SOS's, no reports of wreckage, no life rafts. There's nothing to point to certain disaster and besides, this happens often enough."

"What happens often enough?"

"What we find in these cases, where a yacht is reported overdue, is that the crew has changed their destination," the man says. "We often find them weeks later in a different sea altogether."

"A different sea?" I ask incredulously.

"Yes, you know, the Med."

I have seen the Rock of Gibraltar, its looming rock face guarding the entrance to the Mediterranean.

"That doesn't seem likely," I say. "Leaving the Atlantic for the Mediterranean? You are telling me that sailors do this? Change plans without telling anyone?"

"Yes."

"I just don't believe it. David and Sarah's course was for Madeira, either via the Azores or not. David promised to call as soon as he touched land, anywhere. Even if they had crossed into the Med, they'd have stopped somewhere by now."

"It happens all the time, Miss. Usually they just change their minds, you know, and they head in another direction. Maybe they meet up with some people and they decide to sail together. And sometimes sailors forget that family members are worried about them. They don't always call when they reach port. They don't think like land-lubbers."

"You're suggesting that my brother is drinking beer in some seaside café and hasn't bothered to call?"

"We have cases like this every year."

"I've never heard of this."

"Really, it happens a lot."

"How many do you never find?" I ask. Wandering lost heroes. Fishermen floating face down. Women pacing the shore.

"Now, it's too early to start worrying about that. We are doing everything we can to notify commercial and private vessels, as well as the coastal ports in France, Spain, and Portugal. The Azores, Canaries, Gibraltar, and the coastguards in the Med have been contacted, and, of course, Madeira. Thinking positive is always the best thing to do in these kinds of situations."

David must have been twenty before he even saw the ocean. "If he's out there he's trying to get towards land," I say.

"Listen, Miss, boats are designed to float. Even if they break up, they usually still float and show up on a shore somewhere. There have been no reports of wreckage or abandoned boats. At this point, no news is still good news. Don't worry. It's too early to worry."

When then? How to slow time in this mountain-edged land where the fall migration of birds is almost over?

"When would you suggest I start worrying?" I ask.

"Keep calling us. Try to remember something that might be helpful."

OCTOBER 17. *This is a letter I find in a box of old Christmas cards while you are somewhere in the middle of the Atlantic:*

September 1, 1994
Rowlands Castle, Hants, U.K.

Hi Everybody!!
It's a rainy, cool day here and summer seems to be over, so I finally get a chance to write. Sarah and I have just returned from a two-week sailing holiday down to southwest England. What an adventure! Mugwump *was great, the weather mostly fine, and the wind was abundant though mostly from the wrong direction. What freedom to sail into a quiet bay, drop anchor, and set up*

camp as it were. We had several firsts, including our first night passage, 77 miles out of sight of land. Perfect conditions, a light following wind, and a full moon lighting our way, with Mugwump romping along with "Gertrude" (our self-steering gear) at the helm most of the way, it was magic. Nothing for us to do but sit back and enjoy the ride.

Landfall at Dartmouth in the early hours of the morning was a little nerve-wracking as our electronic navigator said we were in the right spot yet we couldn't make head or tail of the entrance lights. I wasn't sure what to trust: our own eyes or an electronic gizmo, then just as we were about to turn away Sarah made out the lights and we were right on course. Our entrance in the morning mist, with houses perched on the steep sides of either bank, was silent and spectacular. We tried to get further west but strong southwesterly winds drove us back; instead we turned Northeast and visited Brixham and Torquay in beautiful Torbay.

The return passage was not so idyllic as on the way out. We left at 9:00 p.m. in rain and fog with a promising forecast (which soon proved wrong!). The wind was force 6, not so strong, but the seas were large and confused at times. Sarah got badly seasick and because Gertrude couldn't handle the seas I had to stay on the helm all night long. At first I felt a little apprehensive when the log regularly reached 7.5 knots as we surfed down wave after wave. I soon realized Mugwump loved these conditions and began to enjoy myself (Sarah unfortunately did not). The only thing which disturbed our headlong plunge eastward was the odd rogue wave 90 degrees to the rest which seemed to spank Mugwump's hull and soak me. I had convinced myself that the waves seemed bigger coming out of the deep dark night, but the morning light told a different story. I was surprised to find the waves were higher than I expected. After 13 hours on the helm I began seeing things in the clouds and wave crests. Sarah had recovered enough to give me a break. As we neared the quiet bay in which we were to anchor we realized the engine wouldn't start! (due to a fluke electrical fault). Now we had dropped anchor under sail before, but this was a holiday weekend and the bay was full of boats, plus we were pretty tired. After ripping the engine cover off and cursing it for 10 or 15 minutes I managed to hand-crank start it after several attempts. We motored in and dropped to hook, let the sails fall where they may and collapsed in the fore cabin. It felt like we had crossed the Atlantic, not just Lyme Bay, yet we felt like real sailors.

OCTOBER 18. *This is a coastguard's sombre list of the things that could have happened while you are somewhere in the middle of the Atlantic:*

Crew can't recharge the batteries due to engine or wind vane difficulty.

Radio is inoperable.

Bilge pump cannot be powered.

Yacht may be taking in water.

Yacht is dismasted and jury-rigged.

Yacht may be off-course due to poor navigation, an incapable self-steering device, broken rudder, or because crew is sick or dehydrated.

Crew may have changed course.

Yacht has sunk.

Crew is floating in life raft.

Crew is shipwrecked and hurt.

Yacht is drifting towards France, Spain, or Portugal, with or without crew.

Pirates near the African coast.

OCTOBER 19. This is what I promise myself while you are somewhere in the middle of the Atlantic, forty-seven days silent:

I will tell my parents tomorrow.

OCTOBER 20. Mom and Dad know:

My father learns first because he answers the phone.

"Yeah, things just didn't seem right," he says. "Okay, Cath. I'll tell your mother."

"No, Dad. I think it should be me."

"OK, dear. Elizabeth!" The name sounds strange. I rarely think of my mother as having a first name. "Elizabeth, it's Cathy." There. Are we introduced?

She asks about the kids before I have a chance to say anything.

"Yes. Fine," I answer.

She has more questions that require one-word answers.

"No. Yes. Yes. Mom? Yes. Better. No. Mom? Mom?"

"Yes, dear, what is it?"

"I need to tell you something about David and Sarah."

"All right."

My mouth goes dry. "David and Sarah have gone sailing. They've left England and are headed for the island of Madeira."

"Where is that again?"

"South of Portugal."

"Oh yes. I remember."

"No one's heard from them in six weeks, Mom."

I pause. Wait for her voice. The line is quiet.

I take a breath and continue. "The British Coastguard has been contacted. They have designated *Mugwump* overdue, which means that the boat is late in arriving at its intended destination. They don't consider it lost."

"We were wondering why he hadn't called," she says.

"I know."

"I've been worried. But too worried to say anything out loud. I told myself he was too busy to call. That he had a new job. I thought he and Sarah were probably sailing around but I didn't think they'd go so far, so soon."

"Well, that's David," I say. I am immediately guilty for the comment. I am betraying my brother, reducing his choices to mere personality traits.

"I thought about him all the way home from Calgary," says Mom. "It reminded me of the time we came to visit you, just before Victoria was born. David and your Dad in the front seat. We all went to Banff together. Do you remember?"

"I remember."

"How long have you known, Cathy?"

"Awhile. Weeks. I'm sorry I didn't tell you and Dad earlier. I kept thinking that I'd get some news and then I wouldn't have to worry you. But there is no news, and I thought it was time for you to know."

"Yes. You were right to tell us. It was time."

When the phone clicks, I picture a scene unfolding two provinces away in a small kitchen with teapot and clock wallpaper. Dad is cool, not showing any worry, downplaying the seriousness of the situation. He thinks he's protecting her. But Mom is getting furious. *You never worried about these kids like I did*, she yells. *You always let them do whatever they wanted.* This lack of proper discipline is the root of our waywardness, she has often claimed. *I knew this would happen. Sailing,* she spits out the word with disdain. *Crazy.* She slumps down in a chair, crying. *Why did David do this to me?* My father begins to pace and yell.

Get a hold of yourself! His emotions are let loose too. *You're over-reacting. No one's sure of anything.*

I let the scene fade away. They have a right to be angry and fearful. And maybe I imagined it all wrong. Perhaps they hugged each other and talked quietly.

OCTOBER 21. *This is what happens the last time we realized you were missing:*

He borrows Dad's car at eleven in the morning and says he'll be back in awhile. By 5:00 p.m., he hasn't returned, and I begin to make noises—it's my night for the car. Dad phones some of David's friends but Garth, Kevin, and Yak all feign ignorance. But word must have spread amongst the group because an hour later a girl calls and tells us that David has cleaned out his bank account and taken off. She thinks my brother is going to Saskatchewan.

Our family is stunned and silenced, unable to move. It's like watching a boulder roll towards us. We hear the thunder-ing, see it coming, but are unable to jump out of its path—we're glued to the gold, short-pile carpet. My mother speaks first. "Oh, no, what should we do?" she wails. "Why would he run away?" She looks me in the eye. I shrug. *How would I know?* Lately, I haven't paid much attention to my sev-enteen-year-old brother, and I am certainly unaware of his emotional state.

I am surprised, though, at David's lack of imagination for destinations. *Saskatchewan?* The girl must be wrong. He's mak-ing his way west, probably as far as the coast. I wonder if David has girlfriend problems and is eluding some guilt or a broken heart by leaving, but when the girl calls back—her voice gulp-ing when she tries to compose herself—she explains that

David told her he could no longer live in this family. He felt like he was dying.

The secret was out: we were *dysfunctional* before the term was even a word in the popular lexicon of families. My brother's escape proclaimed that there was something not right. He was trapped in the cloud of intense but unnamed feeling that floated in our home—a weighted shadow, a thin shroud threatening to descend and smother us while we flailed against it, like children punching a limp parachute, keeping the skin afloat.

Kerry and Dad are calm as they discuss what could be done. The extent of David's feelings isn't the important thing—just how to get him home safely. They lean their heads together and speak quietly. You'd think they had done this before. My father makes a call to the RCMP. I hear bits of the conversation: "...a minor driving through Saskatchewan. An APB? Do you think that's necessary?" My mother becomes upset when she realizes what Dad is doing. She starts shouting at him while he's still on the phone. "The police will chase the car! Tell them not to chase the car!" She can hardly breathe as she paces.

"Calm down!" my father yells, not bothering to cover the mouthpiece.

Although I'm angry with David for ruining my Friday night plans, I am also fascinated with the getaway that is unfolding—my underage brother, fueled by despair, has raced across a land that is just beginning its short fecund season of grains and grasses. Has he rolled the window down? Is he sticking his head out every few minutes to suck in the wind? Maybe it's Saskatchewan's blue air David needs, Saskatchewan's long roads encouraging him to break free. Or perhaps he wants to flee his loneliness.

Just before midnight, David calls from Regina to say he's sorry. He cries when Dad tells him to stay the night and drive back in the daylight. "Do you have enough money?" my father asks. When my brother gets home, no one says a thing. Our family shrugs. We take another punch at the descending cloud. It stays up and we go on.

OCTOBER 22. *This is what our oldest sister says while you are somewhere in the middle of the Atlantic:*

"I have a bone to pick with you," says Diane on the phone. But I imagine the words, *I have a crow to pluck off you*, and feel hands pulling at feathers until my skin is prickly and raw.

"I don't understand why you felt it was necessary to tell them," says my sister. "It's fine for *you* to share your fears with Mom and Dad, but you're not here to take care of things," she says. "You've alarmed Mom."

The truth *is* alarming, I think, but don't say out loud.

"I understand that this must have been hard for you," she continues, struggling to keep her voice calm. "You didn't want to worry anybody, hoping David would call and no harm done. You were right to tell Kerry and me, and maybe Dad. But there was no reason for Mom to know. She's in such a state now—she can't sleep or eat. She's crying all the time, and you've dumped it all in my neck of the woods. Guess who's going to have to take care of her?"

"He's her son, Di," I say quietly. "She has a right to know."

"The right to know what?"

"To know that his boat is four weeks overdue and that David said he'd call as soon as he arrived either in the Azores or Madeira."

"He's probably forgotten that we even exist."

"No. He promised me." I feel my head shaking. "He promised me that he'd call as soon as he could. He took this voyage seriously, Diane. He planned it for a long time. He's *responsible*."

"Well, that's where you're really wrong, Cath." Her voice is loud and cold. "I think he's extremely irresponsible. Remember India? He didn't call for months."

"That's because nobody can call out of India," I answer, and now I'm yelling. "Besides, David *and* Sarah left explicit instructions with Sarah's mother. If they weren't heard from in three weeks she was to call the coast guard. Are we to imagine that Sarah has forgotten about her family as well? I'm sorry, Diane, but I had to tell Mom. I am doing everything I can think of to find him. She needs to do what she can. Whatever that is. If he were my son, I'd want to know."

I am shaking and confused when I hang up the phone. My sister's reaction was unexpected. It was like we were talking about two different men, each of us claiming to understand his true character. Have I made a mistake? Is David as unthinking as Diane suggests? Or is it the keeping of David's secret that has made me untrustworthy? Perhaps it is my own secretive nature that irritates my sister, the way I never tell her anything first.

My head hurts from trying to determine where my loyalties lie.

Is she right? Should I have shielded our mother even longer and thereby shielded my sister too?

What responsibilities do adult children have towards their parents? Or their siblings? *The right to know what*? Diane had questioned.

I look out the bedroom window. A yellow leaf is clinging to the mountain ash in the front yard. Between the bare

· · · 44 · · ·

branches, the blurred backdrop of the downtown cityscape comes into focus. From this perspective, the towers are not the correct heights and the flat light manipulates the sense of depth. It's like an Escher woodcut where the buildings are impossible and the staircases angle off in weird ways and no matter how you follow a set of stairs up you always find yourself at the bottom.

OCTOBER 23. *This is what the coastguard says when you are missing for 52 days somewhere in the middle of the Atlantic:*

"I think we need a detailed description of your brother," says the man on watch. He pauses. He knows that I know what he's implying.

I was the last one in our family to see David. Does that mean I remember him best? Which details are important?—

- *Just under six feet, 190 lbs.* (lighter the year he ran the New York Marathon).
- *Brown eyes* like Mom's, flashing excitedly during a card game.
- *Thin colourless lips* holding tight against his shame when he brings Dad's car back from his failed escape.
- *Wide ripe Adam's apple* vibrating as he argues with Kerry about a Winnipeg Jets hockey game.
- *Chipped front fluoride-stained tooth* shining in a wide grin the first time he holds Tegan.
- Short chewed fingernails on hands that built a kite too heavy to fly.
- *Orange stubble* grazing my cheek when we say goodbye under grey Scottish skies at the Craignure ferry dock.

"Is this going to help?" I shout at the man on the phone. "When bodies wash up on shore are they even recognizable?"

"Are there dental records available?" he asks.

I am struck again by the power of his questions. A haiku writes itself.

> *the body is gone*
> *enamel of teeth*
> *last to succumb*

"Is there anything else you can tell me?" asks the coast-guard, quietly.

"No," I answer, my voice curt. "There's nothing."

But I see him, age eight, clinging to a corner of the Pan-Am pool, and though his small toes can press against the bottom, he screams at the blue water surrounding him. I paddle around wondering when Mom and Dad are going to let him get out.

OCTOBER 24. *This is where my children think you are, somewhere in the middle of the Atlantic:*

The globe spins wildly on the kitchen table.

My son David keeps it going with his fingertips, the palm hovering over the world like a low cloud. We watch the shapes and colours of continents blur into blue.

"Did you know that the earth is three-quarters water, and only one-quarter land?" I ask him. "And did you know that our bodies are more than half water?" Tegan grabs her thighs and shakes them like Jell-O.

"Tell me again where Uncle David and Auntie Sarah are?" asks David.

"This is where they sailed from, this little corner of Ireland. And here is where they are going." My finger leaves the land-crowded northern latitudes and follows the bulge of the Atlantic. I point to where the globe is worn. The little blue island has been rubbed away, revealing the frayed edges of the globe's paper covering. David picks at it with his nails. We've done this so many times, touched Madeira with our fingertips, and now it's gone.

"You know, they're not dead," Victoria calls from the hallway. Victoria is unable to stay out of any family conversation even if she's not in the same room. "They're on a desert island," she claims firmly as she enters the kitchen. "They got hit on their heads and they can't remember who they are."

Tegan looks at her big sister. "Where?" she asks.

Victoria pulls the globe towards her and looks closely into the ocean. "Here. Here are some islands. A–Z–O–R."

"Azores," I say. "The Azores archipelago."

"See. There are lots of them." Victoria taps the globe repeatedly. "They're on one of those." Tegan reaches for the globe and runs her hands over the surface, feeling for the small rises of land.

"Maybe they don't want to be found," David says. "Maybe they want to live alone on a desert island."

"You mean deserted island," I answer. "Desert is sand, no water. Deserted means abandoned."

OCTOBER 25. *This is what you and I talk about on a May afternoon, two years before you went missing somewhere in the middle of the Atlantic:*

David and I are walking across a moor towards the sea. The gorse is in flower, small pink blooms. A buffeting wind is at our backs. My shoulder knocks against his arm. We talk of our lives, how unexpectedly things have unfolded. David has become a jack-of-all-trades in Fionnphort: construction worker, wannabe boat builder, cook in the town's only pub, and a gardener growing vegetables on a windy rainy slope. He laughs at the way his life has turned out. At one time he had hoped to find work as a deckhand in Australia but now he's in Scotland with an English girl from Nottingham.

I tell him my tales from home, the family dramas that fill my life. There's the time my son threw every thing in Sam's closet—socks, shoes, underwear, starched and pressed shirts, hangers and all—down the second-floor laundry chute. "It sounded like thunder," four-year-old David laughed when I found the pile on the basement laundry floor. On a different day, my brother's namesake peed into the heat vent in his room and later explained, "The bathroom was too far away, Mommy."

"He's brilliant! I love this kid!" David roars. "And your house sounds too damn big."

We laugh as we pick our way along a cliff edge looking for a slot where we can descend to the shore.

"You've mellowed, David."

"Have not," he says, smiling.

"Yeah," I laugh. "I remember the speeches about marriage, children, careers and the dreaded *suburbia*."

"I don't feel any different about the subject. It's just that I don't think about it much here."

"EVERYONE HERE IS WASTING their lives," David preaches in my living room. He is pacing the floor, his face red and his voice almost shouting. "Look at Calgary. Poorly-constructed but cheap houses, arena-styled grocery stores, and shopping malls the size of small towns. Suburbia is softening, thinning your souls. And everyone is the same. No one daring to think that there may be an entire world to move through, not just this sprawling grid of land scraped of all reminders of geography. Really, I don't know how you stand it. I don't know how anyone can live like this."

"This way," David says, and I follow him down through the narrow gaps of giant boulders. The sea is below us, a blue plain, streaked and rippled by the wind.

"I've always wanted to live by the sea, David," I say, clinging to a rock. "I thought I would be by now. We had a chance to move to Vancouver last year but I wasn't sure I could handle the rain. So instead we renovated the bungalow. I'm living in a beautiful house, staying in one place under magnificent Alberta skies, but I'm missing the rest of the world."

"But you're here, seeing my part of the world. There's still hope for you," he laughs. He flings an arm across my shoulder.

"I'm not sure about that. I might be here, but I've left three children at home with chicken pox. I'm not much a traveller anymore. And, apparently, not much of a mother."

"It's chicken pox."

"They'll have scars. I just know it."

"This is it," David says when we jump down to the hard-packed white sand. "My favourite beach."

Our feet don't make a mark as we walk towards the surf where the sea funnels inland between the volcanic rock headlands. Deep waves beat the shore with the regularity of a machine. In the middle of the crescent-shaped beach, we see a woman standing with a red blanket spread at her feet. She is watching two children run back and forth between her and the curling lip of the sea. We hear them squeal into the wind, the sounds of joy and terror.

At the water's edge, David gathers some stones that the tide has left behind. He pulls his shoulder back and then with quick flicks of his wrist pitches the stones like dice. They disappear into a ruffled sea. He kneels down, gathers more stones and fills his pockets. I watch the boy-in-the-man, his half smile a little higher on the right side of his face, his eyes following a shadow passing overhead.

"Shit," David says and starts rubbing his left eye. "Did that bird shit on me?"

"No, there's nothing there. It's probably just sand falling from the wing."

He blinks slowly like he's about to cry and I see his seven-year-old face—two glistening teardrops perched on soft freckled cheeks. I had once found David under the stairs in the fruit room in our house in Winnipeg. His hands, covering his ears, were shutting out our parents' angry words in the kitchen above. I climbed in beside him and we huddled together in the half-dark—the adult despairs and frustrations a mystery to us. Our heartbeats raced together when a pair of shadows came down the stairs, cutting through the slivers of light between the risers. Would we be discovered or forgotten? What was worse? To have our hiding place revealed or live forever under the basement stairs with beets bleeding in fat glass jars and the ice skates we can never tighten ourselves?

"Got it. Whatever it was," David says, taking his hand from his eye.

"Good."

"You know something, Cath. I've been thinking about your life. The way you live, you're risking your present." He takes a rock out of his pocket and weighs it in his hand. "And the way I live, I'm risking my future." He skips the stone into the cold waters of the North Atlantic.

32°38'N 16°54'W

And all I ask is a tall ship and a star to steer her by.

JOHN MASEFIELD

THE PLANE SITS ON the tarmac.

The Portuguese pilot apologizes for the delay in unhurried, broken English. Lisbon is socked in with low clouds. He doesn't know for how long.

I press my face to the small plastic window. Heavy, grey veils shroud the old city. I can't see the wing tip in the falling fog.

Sam and the children watch me pack.

"If you love someone," I explain, "you'll do anything to save them."

Stand on a shore and wave your arms. Call to them. *This way. This way to land.* And for the others you love, the ones who are safe, you will leave them, even to chase a ghost.

"What will you do there?" Sam asks, as I throw shorts, cotton pants, sandals into the bag.

"I'll hand out posters and try to find someone who knows something about *Mugwump.* Maybe a yacht had radio contact with them while at sea."

"OK. But it's been more than a month, almost two."

"I know. Fifty-six days since they left Ireland."

"There may be no boats left in Madeira."

I ignore him while I scrunch up my bathing suit and stuff it into a running shoe. It is a desperate plan but I'm not ready to give up yet.

"You're taking a rock, Mommy?" Victoria asks. She is watching me shove a green turtle-shape into my other shoe.

I had a dream about David and Sarah. While I slept, a sea turtle grew into an island and swam under their boat.

Kerry is worried about me going to Madeira alone.

"Isn't this kind of crazy? What if something happens to you?" he asks me. I hear the unspoken question: *What if you don't come back, either?*

"Somebody's got to go."

"Why?"

"Okay, then. *I* have to. I can't just sit around hoping the coastguard or the Department of External Affairs is going to call with some news."

"What about Mom?"

My mother's reaction is a surprise.

"If anyone should go, it should be you, Cathy."

I loosen my grip on the phone. Have I heard her correctly? I was expecting a passionate plea for me to stay home where it's safe, or at least a vocalized concern about leaving the children, but she brings up none of these things. She asks about particulars. Where I will stay. Who I will talk to. What kind of information I am looking for. Do I have pictures of the boat? David? Sarah?

I realize that my mother is not locked in a state of alarm, working herself into frenzy. She is a woman whose fear is real and is trying to find a way through.

"Does the Canadian Consulate know when you will arrive?"

THE PLANE CLIMBS THROUGH air thick as wool.

The earth spins below.

The winds gather speed in the dark flesh of night.

Over the ocean, the sky is clear, a crown of stars hanging in the heavens. In the east, a quarter-moon rises, a silver scythe on an upward swing.

I imagine my parents here with me, flying over the water, peering into a turbulent sea of white jeering tongues. We are looking for a boat. A white hull and red sail. I don't tell them how afraid I am. How empty I feel.

It's a strange thing to drop out of sky over ocean.

The plane descends into nothingness, only a white slice of moonlight points the way to Africa. And then I see her, a glimmer at first, a single ray, and then a bright floating jewel rising out of the deep. Her sole purpose—to catch us in our fall.

I expect this island to give something up. A man, a woman, a boat.

I expect mountains to fall, spill their cracked boulders into the sea and widen the shore. Land swelling like an ink stain on cotton.

My hand goes to the window. A sister and daughter's fingers reaching for a thousand lights.

Who is lost?

Who will be found, on this chance of land?

THE SOUND CARRIES ON a windy morning. I hear it even before I see the boats—the unmistakable resonance of metal halyards ringing against aluminum masts. It is a sound heard in every harbour in the world. A lament. A revel. God-aimed poles swaying like metronomes.

The marina, in the capital of Funchal, is washed in white light. Sun glints off polished wooden decks and lacquered hulls. Bright silver wires crisscross the air—a web of shrouds and stays and twisted cables.

I shield my eyes from the glare and look for *Mugwump* in the tangle of boats. Perhaps in the night she limped into the harbour.

The marina is tightly packed, like one large deck with over a hundred masts. Boats are rafted to each other four or five deep along a horseshoe-shaped quay, a hundred feet long. The setting reminds me of a jigsaw puzzle we did as children: a painting of a scene along the Thames River. The water was dark. Masts and crosstrees were thin black lines against a reddening sky.

I walk slowly along the quay, reading the names on the hulls, estimating their length. My eyes scan for a body I will know—the broad back, a taut arm. I am looking for his hair, bright in the sunlight, and the form of a dark-haired woman close by.

At a forty-foot ketch, I stop and admire a luminous white hull, glowing like a fresh snowdrift. A blue canvas awning flaps in the breeze. Two masts sway in unison. I rub my toe against a thick plaited painter, knotted on a metal ring. The rope grinds, tightens with the movement of the boat and a heavy feeling tugs inside my chest. My heart, coiled, loosens with longing.

I hold my breath.

Every moment can contain a memory.

SIMON IS STANDING BEHIND me. He arranges my hands on the wheel, inside his own.

"Don't hold on tight, luv. Let it spin through your fingers. Remember, you're not steering the boat. You're finding the wind."

He shows me how to look for luffing along the edge of the sail closest to the mast.

"You want to keep the sail taut. No ripples. No flapping. Just air passing over the canvas. A long, unhindered breath."

The yacht heels hard to port and the crystal-flecked Mediterranean breaks across the deck. Over our heads an ancient sky unrolls like blue parchment.

In the cockpit, my legs shake.

"Well?" Simon asks, after the island of Cos dips behind us into the sea.

"Well what?"

"Do you like it?"

I have to yell to be heard. "I don't feel in control. The boat is moving all on its own, like an animal."

"No," says Simon. "We're the puppet masters here. And the wind is only one of the strings."

I didn't expect this.

The body's memory. The movement in my legs and belly.

I didn't expect the sounds. The chimes. The wind.

Or the light. The scorching, skin-searing brightness, burning away my present life and leaving in its place the desire to remember, and relive.

I know why David wanted this life. The senses are awake.

THE TELEPHONE BOOTH IS on the quay. A plastic half-bubble overlooking a statue of a mermaid.

"When did you arrive?" asks Sam.

"Two in the morning."

"Hotel all right?"

"Fine. What I saw of it in the blur of my exhaustion."

"Here, David wants to talk to you."

"He's up already?"

"Did you find Uncle David, Mommy?"

"No sweetie, not yet."

"Have you seen any dolphins or whales?"

"I'll keep my eye out."

"OK. Bye."

"Put Daddy...." The line goes dead. "...back on."

Oh, well.

I hang up the phone.

I should have told David I saw a mermaid.

I walk over to the stone sculpture. It's an unusual depiction of the mythical sea nymph. She's neither demure nor small like her famous sister the Little Mermaid in Copenhagen. This mermaid is curved and fleshy. Her face is turned to the wind, the mane of hair blown back and hardened in the salt air. But the arms seem out of proportion, longer than her tail. It's like she has raised herself up to appear as large and as furious as possible.

TWENTY-FOUR, TWENTY-FIVE, twenty-six, my steps measure the length of a large yacht moored at the far end of the marina. Round portholes circle the black hull like silver grommets. Two towering masts loom over every yacht in the marina. A British ensign hangs limply off the stern.

"She's sixty-eight feet!" calls a young blond woman, ducking under a gigantic boom. I stop counting at twenty-seven. "*Columban's* a big old thing, but she's got some class."

It's true. She's a bold-looking boat. And she is over twice the length of *Mugwump*.

"I recognize the name," I say to the woman dressed in shorts, deck shoes, and a baggy blue t-shirt. "I mean I know about Saint Columba, the Irish monk. I've visited Iona."

"Oh, yeah? I've never been to that part of Scotland. Well, originally, she was called the *Silver Shamrock*."

"I thought it was bad luck to change a boat's name."

"Stories. The usual rot." She raises her hand, shielding her eyes from the sun that has climbed high in the sky. "Would you like to come aboard?"

I walk across the gangway onto the deck, stepping around a bucket and jerry can. The boat is moving gently. I feel like I am standing on something alive, a slumbering beast of wood and steel. I have missed this feeling.

"My name's Jo, by the way." The woman kicks at a pile of foul weather gear.

I tell her mine and where I'm from.

"A long way from home. England, myself," she says. "Sorry about the mess. This is the end of the season for *Columban*. No more charters this year so I'm slowly cleaning her up, doing some work on her."

"You're crew?"

"No, the crew gets to go home. I'm the bloody captain,"

she laughs. "I get left with all the shit jobs. Would you like a cup of tea?" And with a leap she is gone, down the companionway.

I look around the boat. She is right. *Columban* is in chaos as if the entire contents of the cabins have been hauled up on deck. Towels are drying on the lifelines. Pillowcases and t-shirts hang over a rope stretched between the aft mast shrouds. What looks like a bed sheet is actually a sail crumpled on the boom. The deck is littered with laundry baskets, buckets, and plastic bags but the ropes are neatly coiled and looped in their proper place—the sign of a careful sailor. It is an irony I love. The ocean sailor chooses to cross the most unstable, unpredictable environment on earth, and while the water and wind wreaks havoc on his vessel, he's trying to maintain order. A sailor is often a step behind putting things right or mending the destruction caused by the very elements he is trying to negotiate. And of course, survival depends upon it.

Jo emerges with two mugs and a man in his late twenties. She introduces me to Nick, the son of the owner of *Columban*. He's been helping her with repairs. Nick shakes my hand. Damp blonde curls fall over his forehead. "Are you on another boat?"

"No, I'm trying to find one. My brother's. I'm looking for anyone who may have had radio contact with a yacht called *Mugwump*." I peel a sheet of paper from a thick stack.

Nick leans over Jo's shoulder. They study the poster for a long minute.

"Unusual name," says Jo.

"It means 'fence-sitter,'" I say. "*Mug* on one side, *wump* on the other. But apparently there's also a mugwump tree in New Zealand. David and Sarah loved the name."

"Well, people who've heard it will remember," says Nick.

· · · 58 · · ·

I explain to Jo and Nick the circumstances of *Mugwump's* disappearance and the British Coastguard's broadcasts over the mariner's band but neither has heard anything about the missing yacht.

"Sorry," says Jo. "But I've been in Madeira for over two weeks now and I don't monitor the radio unless I'm at sea."

This is just the first boat, I remind myself—there are a hundred more in this marina. But my face must show my disappointment because Jo says, "Your family must be worried."

Below deck, Jo pours more tea. She moves the mugs aside and spreads the few photos I have of *Mugwump* across the table. The first pictures David sent of his newly purchased boat were taken while she was in dry dock at the Tarquin Yacht Harbour in Emsworth, England. The hull is supported on each side by five rough-hewn logs positioned at a forty-five degree angle. The front edge of the black keel rests on an oil drum. In spite of the crude cradle, the angle of the shot makes her white hull appear long and elegant. In the interior shots, *Mugwump* looks like a classic sailing vessel with polished wooden bulkheads and lockers. There is a small galley with a bench, a fore cabin for sleeping, and a chart table below the radio. The cabin is narrow, maybe six or seven feet across.

"They did a nice job restoring her," says Jo, comparing early and later photos.

David and Sarah bought a new aluminum mast. They protected the keel with layers of blue antifouling paint. The top deck and coach house were sanded and coated in marine enamel and a thin racing stripe was added to adorn the hull. With a new sail cover on the boom and a blue railing cloth stitched with the name *Mugwump* in large white letters, she was done.

"The boat has a long keel," Jo tells me. "It stretches from bow to stern and it's deep. A long keel protects the rudder. Her stern is narrow which is also good. If the sea is running astern, the waves won't wash over the back and swamp the boat. The boat's designed for ocean cruising. She was built to do this kind of sailing." David would agree. She's small but sturdy, he claimed.

My favourite photo is of *Mugwump* at sea. David is standing on the foredeck, his arms outstretched. One hand rests on the original wooden mast, the other grips the shroud, a thick wire that attaches the mast to the hull. Though my brother is upright in the picture, the boat is keeling and the horizon line tilts to the right. *Mugwump* is on a starboard tack, the white jib filled with wind and a gorgeous red-brown mainsail flying before a blue sky. The boat reminds me of a Chinese junk, dark canvas folded like fans.

"Tanbark," says Jo. "That's what they call a red sail. In older times sails were dyed in hemlock or oak bark. The brown tannin protected the cotton from mildew. Today these types of sails are romantic, classic. For the sailor who considers sailing to be an art form not just sport."

THE CLERK AT BILLY's News and Smoke Shop in downtown Calgary slides five glossy magazines into two slim brown paper bags.

"Have fun with that," she says, handing David the packages.

"I intend to," he answers.

Our favourite is *Wooden Boat*, a teasing magazine that subtly implies that piloting anything but a wooden craft may damage your soul. A two-page spread highlighting a sailing yacht built in the fifties makes us swoon. The varnished hull gleams like animal skin. The brass fittings are bright and golden. Below deck, the cabins and galley are luxurious with button-tuck upholstery and bulkheads glowing like fire embers.

"Can you smell the teak oil?" Sarah asks.

"This is almost pornographic," David says. "All I feel is lust."

I fill up three mugs with black tea, careful not to spill on the open pages. I slide a cup to Sarah who is slowly turning the pages of *Pacific Yachting*.

"Wouldn't that one be nice, David?"

"Yes, but nothing beats an original wooden sailing vessel."

"You're a purist, David," I tease. "If you could, you'd grow the tree that would one day become the mast for your boat." I tap the reddish stained windowsill in my forties-era kitchen. "How about fir?"

He laughs. "I think pine grows faster."

I get up from the table when Sarah and David start to talk about specifics: length, hull shape, fittings, berths, weight, sail size. Their heads lean together. They whisper, laugh, even moan over a longed-for attribute.

Eighteen months later, David writes:

The oscillating has ceased! In one week's time we shall jump into "Myrtle the Turtle," drive to Southampton and buy a boat. "By hook or by crook!" Thanks for all the stuff on boats in Canada, but in the end the desire to get a boat NOW! won out. Boats do seem cheaper and better outfitted there, but the trouble of getting there and setting up all over again put us off. We've decided to get a small boat (The Contessa 26) to start off with. It will be less comfortable, but cheaper to buy and run. Simpler to sail yet a very seaworthy boat.

AT FOUR O'CLOCK I thank Jo for the tea and walk to the Customs House on Rua de João. I have an appointment to meet with the port captain of Madeira. Early this morning, I was dragged out of jet-lag-induced sleep by a telephone ringing in my hotel room. *Mugwump* was the first word I recognized, the ending syllable drawn out—*wumppa* vibrating in my ear. The Canadian Consulate in Lisbon had received my fax and had arranged for Mr. Vidigal Aragão to speak to me. I wrote down the address and told the woman I would be able to find it.

The port captain's office is lush, ceremonial, its walls papered in deep red with rows of gold fleurs-de-lys. A broad desk of polished mahogany commands the room like a judge's bench—its surface is bare. A uniformed policeman ushers me towards the black leather chair that faces Mr. Aragão. The captain stands up and shakes my hand firmly. He is dressed in a uniform of navy pants and a blue short-sleeved shirt with epaulets and brass buttons. His skin is smooth, like the bark of an olive tree.

"Welcome to Madeira," he says. His head bows slightly.

"Thank you for seeing me."

"I am sorry that you have come here under such difficult circumstances." His head bows again.

I nod. A fan above the desk spins briskly.

"Please. Have a seat."

The port captain sits down across from me and places his palms flat on the desk. Small tufts of black hair curl across the back of his hand.

"Is there any news?" he asks.

"No. I was hoping maybe you knew something."

"Nothing." He straightens his elbows and pushes away from the desk. Dark crescents of sweat float under his arms.

"We have been aware of your brother's boat for a while now. The British Coastguard notified us three weeks ago that the yacht was overdue. Since that time we have checked the records of all of our entrance ports. *Mugwump* has not arrived in Madeira, at least not officially."

"What about the other islands?" I ask, fumbling in my bag for a map of the archipelago, then spreading it across his desk. "Are they inhabited?"

"This is Porto Santo," he says, putting his finger on an island that is north of Madeira. "Many people live there and some sailors visit. These islands, Ilha Chao, Ilha Deserta Grande, and Ilheu de Bugio? They are rock. Covered in birds." He leans towards me, fingertips pressing together. "I do not think they could be there."

"Couldn't they have come ashore, unseen?"

"You mean in a life raft?"

"Yes."

He shakes his head. "Those islands are remote but they are visited. Scientific people. Bird watchers. Your brother and his girlfriend would be found."

"Yes, of course," I say sharper than I intend. I fold and unfold the map three times before I find the original creases and reduce the paper to a small rectangle. The room is hot and my head is spinning. A buzzing sound swells in my ears.

"Are these the posters you have made?" Mr. Aragão is pointing to a small stack of paper I have placed on the corner of his desk.

I reach for a sheet. David and Sarah's faces flutter like a silent movie reel. He has to take the poster from my fingers because my hand is shaking.

He looks down at the black and white photograph. "They are a nice looking couple, I think."

"Yes."

"Has Falmouth mentioned anything to you about storms in the Bay of Biscay?"

"They said there was nothing out of the ordinary."

"Good. Tropical distubances move north in the autumn and the waters can be rough. But your brother was sailing in early September. A week to cross the Bay. Another week down the Portuguese coast. They should have been fine." His voice sounds hot and thick, like dust blowing through an open window.

They should have been fine.

He looks away from my face for the first time, glancing to the window where thin venetian blinds are pulled closed. Red slivers of sunlight glow under the metal slats.

"Many things can go wrong at sea," he says softly. "But if they are still alive, and on the ocean, there are only two possibilities. Either the boat is jury-rigged or they are in a life raft. In either case, they are probably drifting. Currents could carry them towards Europe, Madeira, the Canary Islands, even the Caribbean. In any of these circumstances, they would have to be found by a passing ship."

"So, luck," I say.

"Yes."

"Do you think there's any hope for their survival?"

"There is always hope."

I leave the port captain at the gates of the Customs House and enter a sepia-toned street scene. Sidewalks are crowded with people—soft-edged faces out of focus rush past. Dusk is falling like ash. Another day gone.

I walk along Avenida Do Mar where buses wait under the swaying fronds of palm trees. The shuddering yellow blocks of metal and glass spew diesel fumes into the crowd. I see a young woman walk slowly around the dark clusters of bodies, her eyes scanning the bus destinations: Camacha, Santo da Serra, Curral das Freiras. A small sleeping child is tied to her back with a length of cotton. Thin brown legs dangle, weighted by shoes, small and white like eggs. When she finds the right line, the woman leans over and puts her brown hardback suitcase down. The child's head slides forward, slips under the fan of her long black hair. I move closer to catch a glimpse of her face. I wonder if she, too, feels the abandonment of the day.

The line starts to move. The man in front of the woman trembles as he reaches for the chrome railing. His white cotton shirt is stained with sweat, a dark V marks his back. When he lifts his foot I see the augmented shoe, a black platform of six inches. He drags the box slowly over the lip of each step. When the woman follows him onto the bus, her arm reaches behind and grips her child. In the shifting of limbs, the mother turns her head and catches my gaze. Her face opens to mine— a smile curving under almond eyes—and with no aspect of loneliness she boards the bus.

I long for the weight. A body tied to mine.

WE HAVE BEEN LOST before. David and I.

We are three and five, holding hands and walking in a store with yellow walls. We don't look much like a brother and sister. He glows like a fat golden cherub while I am a dark, chimney sweep of a girl.

We follow Mom's floral dress down a long aisle, the gathered skirt swinging back and forth like a bell. Passing by a bin filled with coloured flip-flops, I insist we stop to try a pair on. I show David how to pull his big toe away from the second toe so the thong can slip in between. Out of the corner of my eye I see our mother walking away. The yellow blossoms on her dress are fading, the green foliage darkening. I don't chase after her because of a strange pleasure trembling in my belly. Like the beat of a bird's wings. The smaller my mother becomes the more the bird flutters. The sensation only stops when the garden of fabric turns a corner, the pleated fan of her dress clicks closed, and she is gone.

David looks up at my face, wiggles his fingers in my hand, and lets me lead him to the end of the aisle where I am certain she is waiting. The thongs flap loudly as we pad along the linoleum tile.

When she isn't there I don't let go of him. I don't let go when a clerk takes us to the back of the store, gives us cookies, and announces our names over the P.A. system.

"It never happened," my mother claims. "What kind of mother loses her children?"

But I see it in my mind.

"I think I did it on purpose," I try to explain. "It felt physically exciting to see you walk away."

"Well, that makes no sense to me at all. Why would anyone want to be lost?"

I don't know.

THE SEA, THE SEA

They say the sea is cold, but the sea contains the hottest
blood of all, and the wildest, the most urgent.

D.H. LAWRENCE

SLEEP ABANDONS ME IN the early hours of the morning, flee-
ing the storm inside my head. Perhaps it runs along the quay
like a skittering rat.

I wake to familiar smells: damp bog-rot, orange-scented
teak oil, the heavy stench of diesel pressing in the upper
recesses of my nose, and the metallized sweat of a former lover.
I feel Simon's fingertips touching the back of my neck, his soft
English accent whispering in the morning. *You all right?*

I open my eyes and look around: slatted floor, panelled
bulkheads, a narrow cabin door with rounded corners—

a cocoon of wood with one black porthole lifted like an eye patch. I stretch full length in the bunk until my toes press against the wall. I just fit into this space. The sounds of the marina float through the open hatch like an orchestra warming up its strings and percussions. A twisted rope strains on a mooring ring. Halyards and masts ring like bells. Seagulls cry then grow faint.

A breeze blows his scent into my mouth.

Simon is at the helm. I am watching his face as he gives instructions on raising the jib. "That's it. Keep winching." His hand brushes a long brown strand of hair from his eyes. The tattooed dragon on his forearm stretches a wing.

Turkey is to stern, the ancient ruins of Ephesus—stone streets, a library, the brothel returned to the past. We are trying to catch a breeze coming off the island of Samos. I feel the wind gathering as I haul the sail upward, a white triangle broadening, cutting into the porcelain sky. The jib tightens, its centre distended, and *Lady Papillon* shudders and picks up a little speed. As the yacht heels, the waters of the Aegean fall away like a torn scar. I return to the cockpit and slide in beside Simon. With an eye on the horizon and a hand on my thigh, he leans over and kisses me. He tastes like the tempered steel of a blade.

We want to believe it is love that shapes our destinies.

I PICK UP THE phone to make a collect call and then replace the receiver. I'm staying on a boat with a woman captain, I'll explain. That can't worry Sam too much. Nick is leaving today so it will just be Jo and I.

"Can you hear me all right? I'm in that phone booth on the quay."

"There's a small echo but it's okay," says Sam. "Have you learned anything?"

"No. But the port captain is checking all the harbours again. And now that I'm staying in the marina, I'll be able to see every new boat that arrives."

"What do you mean you're staying in the marina?"

"A British woman has invited me onboard a boat she captains. She's alone and says she could use the company."

"That's generous."

"I think she feels bad. About David and Sarah. She wants to help."

"So there's no phone where I can reach you."

"No."

"I want you to phone every second day," Sam insists.

There are demands in families. Parental, sibling, and marital expectations can be veiled or bare. A loved one pleads for recompense: here are the scars, the ones you made—now do not abandon me.

"Have you talked to Diane yet?" I ask.

"Yeah. She's hopeful. She believes David and Sarah are going to survive this."

"Through adversity...our strengths are called forward."

"What?"

"It's something Di believes in."

IT IS DAVID WHO tells me that Diane's first child, Mark, still isn't moving.

"At first the doctors called him a floppy baby, it happens after some deliveries, but now...I don't know," he says in a phone call from Winnipeg. "Brain damage? Nerve damage? No one is sure what's wrong with him."

When I cry with the news, David chastises me. "How can

you be sad about the birth of a new life? Mark will have his time on this earth, for as long and as fully as fate decides."

"You're not imagining what it's going to be like for Diane if he's disabled," I say to him.

"So we shouldn't be celebrating Mark's life?"

"Our sister's life might be forever changed. Diane will help her son thrive, no one will do this job with more intelligence and care—but at what cost to herself, and her freedom?"

"You don't think that maybe Diane's life could thrive because of this?"

"Would yours, David?"

"Yes. I would make sure of that."

But in spite of David's optimism for Mark's life, my brother doesn't stick around to be an uncle to him.

"It's a bugger when engines quit for no apparent reason," Nick says, turning over in his hands the postcard David mailed from Ireland. "They absolutely needed to have the engine working well. It charges the batteries for the bilge pump and the radio. The radio provides weather reports as well as a link to the rest of the world. Feeling connected can mean a lot to a sailor's psyche."

We are sitting around the table in *Columban's* large salon. The sun is pouring through the open companionway, a square of blue sky floats above. An assortment of packed bags are up on the deck—mine, ready to move to a cabin below, and Nick's, destined for a flight to Lisbon.

Nick reminds me a little of Simon—tanned, lean, a fairer version. Simon was taller but the accent is similar. I smile at Nick's white t-shirt—clean, rippled with soft wrinkles, a deep crease across the middle where the shirt dried on a lifeline. Nick clears everything off the table and reaches behind the salon bench to a narrow shelf where the sea charts are kept. He unrolls them like scrolls, palms sliding outward to the torn edges. We place books on the corners. The maps are yellowed like artifacts from the Middle Ages—all that is missing are the four winds blowing in the corners and S-backed sea monsters riding the waves.

We look under the ocean.

I am mesmerized by the cartographer's looping lines—inky fingerprint impressions or a sculptor's last faint touch. The whorls indicate where either the sea floor is falling away at the coastlines or rising up into flat-topped *mesas*—wide shelves of silt shifting with ocean waves and currents. There are so many points where land hovers just below the surface.

Nick explains that the Azores archipelago straddles the Mid-Atlantic Ridge, a part of a rift valley that snakes through every ocean bed. It's like a seam line holding the parts of the world together. The Azores, a chain of nine islands, is where the North American, Eurasian, and African plates meet under the ocean. Out of view of geologists and sailors, the plates shift on a bed of soft, thick mantle, causing earthquakes, tidal waves, and volcanic eruptions. This is how sea beds and islands change.

Nick shows me *Mugwump's* probable route. His finger navigates a path, setting a course over the secret land below. His wrist bone follows like a white moon. The blond hairs on his arm catch the sunlight.

"They may have encountered strong winds and short seas here," he says, tracing a line just outside the Bay of Biscay where the Atlantic Ocean has taken a bite out of France. "The Atlantic is still shallow and high winds can double the size of the waves. It can make for a very rough ride with a strong northwesterly."

"But isn't this further east than they should be?" I ask.

"It depends. When your brother and his girlfriend decided to give the Azores a miss, they would have plotted a route closer to the continent to make better time. And once they're on the water they might realize what a long way it is from Ireland to Madeira. If it gets rough or there's a storm, sailors will often head towards Spain or Portugal. You can only take so much of a heavy sea. It's just too hard on the body and mind."

His hand slides over the paper. I see a twisted rope running through palms, corroding the flesh.

"This is the edge of the continental shelf," says Nick.

My eye follows the long line that separates the northern and southern halves of the Bay of Biscay. South of this line, the sea bed is diving away: a hundred metres, 1,000 metres, 4,000 metres.

"When the winds are fair the waves will become longer in the deep water and the boat isn't tossed around too much. But if there's a northwest gale, and the Bay of Biscay is notoriously stormy, then the boat is forced to run downwind with a following sea. Waves coming from behind can break over the stern and swamp the boat or drive the bow under. Following waves also make it difficult to steer in. In a big sea, the waves can lift a hull so high the rudder will come out of the water and the boat can swing broadside."

I see the waves stepping towards France and Spain, steep green walls marching upon a small boat, spilling over the transom. As the boat falls forward, the mast pierces the black gloom. Was this how it was for *Mugwump*?

I let my arms glide over the coated paper and then like a tired child, place a cheek against the chart—it is dry and cool to my touch, a relief from the fever in my head. I lie quiet, my skin in danger of igniting paper.

"Tea?" Nick asks.

I watch him slide out of the bench. The long muscle of his forearm tightens as he pours scalding water into a chipped pot.

It's too hot.

I close my eyes but see the mapmaker's lines converging and spinning.

A wave breaks over the chart and rushes into the salon.

There's too much water.

The mind cannot fathom such a sea.

A hand shakes my shoulder.

Someone is saying my name.

"Cathy!" Simon calls across *Lady Papillon's* deck. "Let's try the spinnaker!"

He hauls the sail bag out of the forward cabin and attaches it to the bowsprit. He clips the spinnaker's ring onto the halyard and shows me how to pull it up. The sail is barely out of the bag when it begins to move as if alive, twisting with urgency and longing. Like a child's hand searching Santa's sack, the wind grabs at the nylon with impatience. The spinnaker rises, twisting itself into a tall golden pillar. It untangles slowly—the air smoothing the creases like a hand across a bed sheet—then opens to a sudden inferno. It is a piece of the sun, fallen to earth.

I stand under the blaze and watch the air currents shimmer across the surface like flames. Simon and I had put a skin on the wind and it was on fire.

Memory is taunting me.

I negotiate with her, offer some thread to run with but then I pull her back. I am willing to remember, I say, but I must go home again. Your enticements will not work. I have Love. Family. You have only Beauty.

But without mercy she spills the stories she has never forgotten. She gathers the past, makes me look back—what have
you forgotten that you once loved, that you knew to be true?
She traps my memories in a web and lets them out slowly—
the smooth grain of a teak table, the morning sun glancing off
a sail, the wind ruffling the sea's skin. She wants to mesmerize
until I am spent.

When the wind starts gusting, Simon says we have to bring the
sail down.

He leaps across the deck to the bow where the spinnaker
is twisting, trying to free itself from the forestay like a caught
bird. He pulls it into his arms and holds the trapped wind
against his chest. I go below deck into the forward cabin
with instructions to be ready to haul the sail in through the
hatch.

"Here it comes!" Simon calls down to me.

The world goes quiet while the spinnaker cascades onto
my head.

"The sky is falling!" I yell back, but in fact it's more like
pouring sunshine. The yellow cloud slides over my face and
arms. I try to get a grip on the nylon so I can stuff it into the
bag, but it slips through my fingers. It breathes and puffs
around me. It is liquid. Mercury. I can't hold it in my hands.

Simon finds me laughing under the fallen spinnaker. The
sail is spread throughout the cabin, flowing like a silk gown. I
can't stop smiling at the glorious mess I have made.

"Sorry. I just couldn't get a hold of it. It was like trying to
grab air."

Simon finds a clew and starts stuffing. I put my hand on
his arm.

"Wait. Look. It's like a yellow river."

I want to hold time, consider the accidental beauty of a spilled sail.

Simon sits down beside me on one of the narrow bunks. He puts his arm on my shoulder and says, "I need this hatch clear. And if we leave the sail, it could get torn or damaged."

I reach for the bag and we pour the spinnaker back in.

EVERY MORNING I PACE the quay with posters and photographs.

I stop in at the Marina Office first and check for messages on the cork board. If there are sailors standing at the counter I ask them to carry the news of *Mugwump* to the Canaries, the Cape Verde Islands, and the Caribbean. And then I begin my walk. Shielding my eyes from the blinding gleam of boat decks, I scan for the small raised wooden coach house and a thin blue line painted on a white hull. I look for the name.

Please. Let her be here.

There are so many boats. Only one missing?

Morning is the best time to find sailors on their yachts. Securing ropes, retying fenders. Damp bedding is draped over the lifelines. The anchors are checked for drag. I note the moorings of the newly arrived and climb over the rails to talk to the crew. Many are familiar with the poster but can offer no information. They shake their heads while hauling on a mooring line. Most are sympathetic. They pour me tea, coffee, or a beer below deck in wood-panelled cabins. On chart tables, ships' logs are peeled open, eyes searching for the name *Mugwump* in hand-written entries dating back to September—might there be a notation of radio contact? Navigational maps are unfurled, spread across the table. I follow the cracked fingertips showing me routes from Penzance ($50°12'$ N $5°54'$ W),

Brest (48°23' N 4°29'W), Horta (38°32' N 28°38'W), Viana do
Castelo (41°41' N 8°50' W). Sailing is full of risks, I'm told
repeatedly. But the danger seems benign here—the greasy
waters of the marina slap lazily against the hulls.

"It's a long way," says a sailor sitting in the cockpit of a gleaming white yacht. His eyes almost disappear into the soft pink
flesh of his face. "Twelve hundred nautical miles. Too bloody
far. Most people try to break up the trip, calling into Spain or
Portugal before heading down to Madeira. It was an ambitious
undertaking for your brother, I think. Two weeks at sea is too
long. But hell, you can't talk sailors out of anything they have
their hearts set on. People do crazy things cause they love it."

On a forty-foot sloop with a broad wooden deck, I bring
out the photographs of *Mugwump*. A man holds the photos in
his calloused fingers. The Kodak paper curves and the corners
are starting to fray. I explain what Jo has said about the deep
keel. "It doesn't matter one bit," he concludes. He gives the
photos back, leans away from the chart table and tucks his
hands behind his neck. "Long keel or short, small boat or big,
four crew or one. It's the Lady of Fate. It's all luck. Storms don't
always beat the sailor. Sometimes it's whales, or being run over
in the middle of the night by a merchant vessel. Small yachts
can run into floating containers. Of course these things don't
happen very often but they can and do. It comes with the
lifestyle."

When I ask another sailor about the possibility of hitting
a whale, he opens a sea chart for the Bay of Biscay and taps its
surface vigorously. "I've seen whales here, here, and here," he
says. "Pilots. Lots of them. There's minke out there too. And
fin. Even sperm. It's an amazing thing to come upon a pod
breaking the surface. It's a reason to cross the Bay. But running

into a whale? I don't think it's very likely but some people claim it's true."

Drifting containers are the other silent killers of the sea. Large metal cubes, ten to forty feet in length, can be swept off the decks of freighters during storms. They float just under the surface like sea mines. I hear the same story twice about an eighty-foot yacht that went down on a clear star-filled night. The hull broke open and it sank in less than a minute.

But the danger I hear most often repeated, is the chance of being hit by a container ship. "This is where your luck runs out if you had any to begin with," a man tells me, chuckling lightly. His lips, too large for his face, are red and moist. "With modern radar and navigating technology, ships and container barges don't maintain visual watch. No one sees a boat if it crosses their path. No one notices the crush of a small hull. Your brother and his girlfriend could have been the victims of a hit-and-run."

David had mentioned in a letter, last July, that during the crossing from Ireland to Scotland, a huge ship came out of the mist on a collision course with *Mugwump*. David had made a quick tack, but he was uncertain whether the ship had seen them. *It's troublesome,* he wrote.

Danger is always lurking, the sailors tell me. Severed masts, broken rudders, fire and smoke overwhelming a crew. And then there's the water—it's all around and wants to come in. Small yachts usually have only one bilge pump powered by batteries. If the seas are heavy and the pump fails, it takes only half an hour for a boat to fill and flip.

"Don't get into a life raft until you have to step up to it," a man in his late sixties advises as the sun dips behind the mountains. "That's the rule. You're always safer in a boat than a life raft. Of course, if the boat's going down fast, you'd better hope that the raft is ready." His irises catch the last rays of the day and hold the colour between salt-crusted lashes. "Did you know that crews on night watch always hook themselves on, even if the weather is calm? Solo sailors don't bother with tethers. If they're tossed overboard there's no one to help."

Is there a more vulnerable activity in the world than ocean sailing?

"I don't like people much. I prefer the sea," says a dark, muscular man. "But you? You must be lonely here." I remove his hand from my knee.

My loneliness should be irrelevant.

"I'm GOING TO HOOK you on," Simon shouts into the wind.

He grabs the front of my foul weather suit, clipping one end of a tether to a hook on the jacket and the other to a safety eye bolted into the cockpit. "I don't want you to float away from me." He smiles as he says this, his eyes bright, but my face must look stunned. "Just a precaution, luv. You can move around. You'll just have to unhook and re-hook."

"But you're not clipped on, Simon."

"I need to be able to move quickly if something happens."

Ten minutes later, the sky closes in and we sail into a fury.

I sit next to Simon as he steers through the storm. The chrome wheel runs between his calloused palms. *Slide, grip, open, seize.* His hands are like two birds trying to land on a moving wire.

When columns of white spray shoot up like whale spouts, Simon reefs in the mainsail and starts the motor. He keeps the boat at a ninety degree angle to the sea's short waves. The hull slams hard into the narrow troughs. The rigging shudders, carrying a vibration along the deck like electrical pulses.

I don't move.

Eight hours, Simon had estimated this morning when we left Samos under blue skies and a soft breeze. When I ask him now how much longer, he says, "It'll depend on what lies ahead."

I close my eyes, shutting out rain that's as hard as buckshot, and try to imagine the island we are headed for. Naxos. Green meadows, streams, mountains. A notable place in Greek mythology: the sandy shores where Ariadne, the Princess of Knossos, slept and changed her fate.

In the famous myth of the Labyrinth and the Minotaur, we remember Theseus, the hero with the ball of yarn who kills the half-bull, half-man monster. But his success is due to a woman's ambition. Ariadne, the daughter of King Minos, who hires Daedalus to build the perilous labyrinth, devises a plan to gain her freedom from her father's kingdom. She strikes a bargain with Theseus. She will tell him how to escape the labyrinth if he promises to take her to Athens as his future bride. Theseus agrees and Ariadne's unravelled thread guides him out of the maze. True to his word, Theseus flees Crete with Ariadne, but when the ship stops at Naxos, the woman who has saved him disembarks and falls asleep on a beach. Ariadne wakes only in time to see Theseus sail away without her.

Waves are crashing against *Lady Papillon's* hull while I consider the dilemma of this myth. Is the heroine neglected or forgotten? And what about our hero? Now freed, does he willingly ignore his promise, having little concern for the ruin he leaves behind? Or does he keep sailing for Athens because the winds won't let him turn around?

Simon's hand grazes my cheek. I open my eyes and see the ship's wheel spinning in a silver blur. My stomach folds in two and rises to my throat.

Myths are powerful because they fulfill our desire for imagination, truth, and even reinvention. Perhaps Ariadne is the creator of her own fate. Our heroine sleeps on shore because sailing makes her sick.

"HOW EXPERIENCED WAS YOUR brother?" asks an Irish woman.

"He and Sarah have only had *Mugwump* two years," I say. "They've sailed along the southern English coast. Last spring they went up the west coast of Ireland to Scotland."

"That's a lovely trip."

"I'm not sure whether that makes for a lot of experience but my brother's smart and strong. A clear-headed thinker." *I need to believe this.*

"That's good," she says comfortingly.

"Well, it doesn't really matter whether he's experienced or not," her husband adds, after joining us up on the deck. "It's not that hard a trip."

"It's 1,200 miles," I say.

"But the Portuguese trade winds make it easy. Lisbon to Madeira in less than four days." His lined face ripples, skin crushed around the eyes. "I think they're all right, don't you?" he says with an Irish lilt.

No. But I can't say the word. "I just don't know."

"Well, here's what I think. Don't give up. If I was out there, it would be unbearable to imagine no one hoping for my survival."

Women expected to keep vigil from shore.

Most of the sailors I meet are humbled by the power of nature, but not necessarily a God. I hear no words of religious faith, only an acceptance for the oceanic realm of the unpredictable. The men use a feminine language invoking the all-powerful Female, the *other* who is a mystery. The ocean is *She*. The boat is *She*. And Fate is *She*. Even the most brutal of storms have women's names.

I have come to believe that many male sailors subscribe to no philosophy other than, *What will be will be*. They easily accept that they cannot know the sea and that this lack of certainty is no deterrent to setting out. They seek the unknown. For its limits and accompanying fear.

"Really, it's all about physics," a man explains to me, starting his description of sailing with a scientific approach. "Each boat has certain design factors that affect how it responds at sea. Weight, beam, length of keel, displacement, and overall construction. Nature adds the other variables such as currents, swells, wave height and length."

But even his dispassionate explanation starts to crumble when he speaks about human forces set against the physical laws of the natural world. His eyes get brighter, the voice builds like an orator's and I see the pulpit. "Bravery is the deciding factor," he carries forth. "The willingness to test skill against the chances of weather, to be uncertain and confused, and to take a best guess when there is no clear choice."

A best guess.

I have spent hours talking to Jo about boats and sailing and I have not yet seen in her the same kind of passion that runs through the men. Is she more precise, less fatalistic? Does a female sailor's best guess come from a different part of the brain? Are they less willing to take chances at sea and are they less likely to die?

I think women are not the romantic ones when it comes to sailing.

WHEN THE AEGEAN SEA boils over *Lady Papillon's* deck, I slide open the hatch and climb down to the salon. My foot reaches

the last rung, the boat breaches to starboard, and I go with it
into a corner of the table. I try to get up but my balance is off.
From my back, I look through the small square opening and
see Simon grappling with the wheel. His face is happily furious. Behind him the rain drives hard out of low clouds.

Once standing, I grab the metal handle and force the hatch
closed. The high-pitched whine of the wind is finally muffled
but now I can hear the hull slam into the waves, a dull thud
with each drop.

I had hoped I'd feel better below deck, out of the wind
and the rain and the black sea, but the salon feels like a cage
without an exit and without air. I realize that I am under the
water now too. I put my head down on the table but the pitching makes me slide back and forth across the smooth wooden
surface. Through the portholes I catch a glimpse of a dark line
coming in and out of view, the far-off delineation between sea
and sky. I try to recall the solution for seasickness: is it staring
at the horizon line or putting your head between the knees?

"THERE ARE PROCEDURES, MA'AM," the coastguard in
Falmouth repeats over the phone. "Two broadcasts is standard
unless there's new information." His voice is cold and officious.

"I'm asking for a favour here, sir. One more broadcast," I
plead. "They could still be alive. You know there are stories of
survivals. For seventy-six days sailors have been known to survive on the Atlantic."

"Yes, but that's unusual, ma'am."

"Then tell me about *usual* survivals. What exactly would
be *usual*?"

"I think it would be best if you stopped calling us." The
voice sounds far away like he's holding the phone with a
straight arm.

"What?"

"There's really no point in contacting us again."

"Are you kidding me?"

"I am perfectly serious. Please don't call unless you have something new. And of course, we shall contact you if anything turns up."

I have been treading water for weeks, trying to hold up the hopes of two families. The abandonment of an official agency, the Maritime Rescue Coordination Centre of the North Atlantic, is devastating. These are the men who had supported and sometimes even encouraged us in the belief that *Mugwump* may be damaged but the crew not necessarily lost.

I hang up the phone and lean my head against the plastic dome of the telephone booth.

What will I tell my parents in my next call to them?

The boat really has sailed off the edge of the world, Dad.

No living soul has seen it, Mom. Few know it's even missing.

Or, I can't begin to tell you all the things that can go wrong on an ocean. And truthfully, *Mugwump's* chances of being sighted are infinitesimal.

By the way, the British Coastguard think Sarah and David are dead.

It's been too long.

I'm sorry.

My brother had once dared say to me, "You're not the woman you used to be."

Three children, a house, an expired passport was not a life, he claimed.

I didn't argue with him on that day. I didn't call him an asshole. I didn't say that maybe he was disappointing me.

Where was his compassion, his uncertainty? Replaced by empty bravado?

Today, I want to tell him he's not the man I thought he was.

I want to shout across the marina—you should have had a bigger boat—you should have had an emergency locating device—you should have had more crew—you should have reported your position regularly—you should have waited until you had more experience—you shouldn't have been so fucking brave, because you're not here and I'm the one left trying to figure out how to explain what's happened to you.

Let it go, a voice says. *We went sailing, that's all. Shit happens.*

But the shit happened to us, David.

THE MARINA IS JUMPING. Every mast in motion.

At the far end of the quay, *Columban* looms like an ancient galleon, black hull indistinct from the water, the rigging silver in the moon's light. I imagine sails flying from the tall masts, thin and pale like torn veils.

I find Jo half-submerged in *Columban's* engine cavity. A beam of light flies across the cabin, an apparition escaping from the bilge. "Any news?" she asks brightly, flashlight in hand. I shake my head. *Columban* creaks and rolls. A wave slaps at a porthole.

I slide onto the bench, limbs heavy as poured cement, and watch Jo work. It's easy to imagine this twenty-something English woman captaining the sixty-eight foot *Columban* across the Atlantic, blond hair flying like a Scandinavian Valkyrie.

"The boats are really rolling out there," I say.

"Could be the last waves of a spent storm. Madeira is the first bit of land for thousands of miles so they break here."

I stand up, climb a few rungs and look out over the marina. The boats are being tossed like they're made of balsa wood. I wait for a breeze to sweep my face, yet there is none, and the water, too, skinned in black oil, appears solidly calm. But there is some unseen ripple that starts these vessels rocking. A hidden wave. A finished storm.

Jo laughs as she heaves herself out of the hold. "My body was not designed to go down holes that size." She wipes the grease from her hands with a rag.

"You all right?" she asks.

"I just got off the phone with a coastguard in Falmouth. I explained that other than from the posters I've been putting up, no one is aware that *Mugwump* is missing." I pick up a sticky deck of cards on the table. They shuffle in clumps, the paper swollen from the damp air. I throw them onto the table. "I got kind of angry. I might have sworn at him. Anyway, they've asked—or rather instructed—me to stop calling them."

"I'm sorry," Jo says.

"It was a long shot to come here. Pretty naïve."

"No. It's a good thing to hope, to not give up."

I put my head in my hands.

DROWNING IS A PLEASANT way to go.

According to those who have been plucked from the depths at the very last moment, it is the kindest of near-deaths. Sounds are dulled. The mind becomes sleepy. A relaxed airway allows the lungs to fill slowly with water, silt, small bits of seaweed. Just like a boat, the water finds a way in—through cracks and seams, into flesh.

Physiologically, seasickness is a condition where the fluid in the ear's semicircular canals moves with the body's motion. The fluid stimulates the brain receptors that produce headache, dizziness, and vomiting. Seasickness is also an experience that mimics emotional uncertainty. Unable to stand, visually focus, think clearly.

What the hell am I doing here?

Simon slides open the hatch and calls to me.

"Naxos is coming into view!"

I look up at my sailor framed in the open hatchway. He's a man in love with his work. Eyes streaked like marbles. Salt crystals dried on his face. He swings down into the salon, apologizing for the tossing sea like it's his fault.

"Sorry about that," he says, picking up the kettle, some cutlery, and a mug that has rolled to the floor. "The seas were short because of the wind. It made for a rough ride but not dangerous."

But I had seen my fear and I knew it would not negotiate with the unpredictable nature of the sea.

We put away the sails, coil the ropes, and tidy the galley. And then we lie down on the small bunk of our cabin. Under the damp sheet, I take Simon's limp hand and place it on my belly. In his sleep, he strokes my skin. He touches the small bruise on my left breast. The boat and the sea have left their mark, a thumbprint on the place where I faltered.

AT THE APOLO RESTAURANT, tables are pushed together to accommodate a large group of sailors who are celebrating their arrival on the island. This must be an old ritual. For five hundred years seafarers have indulged on this fortuitous rise of land: the fruits of a temperate climate—mangoes, avocados, bananas, figs; sweet pastries and wine; a local beer shared with a stranger who crossed the same sea. After days of three-hour watches, it must be a relief for sailors to sit leisurely over a meal, the air smelling of jasmine instead of brine.

This afternoon, Jo invited me to join her at the restaurant. She had met a couple of Englishmen on the quay and agreed to meet them for a drink around eight.

"Thanks," I said to her. "I'll come. But I'm not going to

explain why I'm here in Madeira. Telling this story is exhausting me."

It's hard to watch a listener's face change—from curiosity to sadness then compassion. The head shakes slowly and sometimes a ripple of relief shows. *There but for the grace of God....*

Jo introduces me to the English sailors. John, from London, and Giles, a Liverpudlian, make a place for me between them.

"I am so glad to be on land," says Giles. He swallows a beer with his mouth and throat open. "You have no idea."

"Yes, our little cruise hasn't been quite as much fun as we hoped," says John.

They both laugh yet don't seem amused.

They tell me they paid to be part of a crew, a sort of adventure cruise and boat-delivering junket that's sailing from England to the Canaries with a stop in Madeira.

"I think we were had, mate," Giles laughs. "They should 'a bloody paid us for all the grief we've put up with."

"Cheers to that," John says and lifts his beer. "So much for the romance of sailing."

"What boat are you on?" asks a man sitting a few chairs away. He leans forward, tucks a few strands of long streaked blond hair behind his ears.

I hesitate and then mumble, "*Columban.*"

"You are together?" he says, his pointed finger swinging between Jo and I. "Two women on a boat?"

I shift my weight on the wooden chair. Jo interrupts the questioning by ordering more beer from the waiter she has called over from the other side of the restaurant. I turn my attention to the far end of the group where a chunky sunburned sailor is telling a story about his yacht's run from Viana do Castelo to Madeira. "Bad weather, but great sailing. " His paunch shakes under a tight white t-shirt. "The wind was fast and furious on the stern. I was rolling in the jib and standing in water up to my waist!"

Jo leans over and whispers, "They probably put up all their sails and let the boat fly. It can be dangerous if the sea is running behind, but certainly fun."

Another man with a thick accent tells his story: A week ago his yacht was sailing in dense fog off the French coast near Ouessant. Visibility was poor so he ran all the lights and tried to peer through the pea soup. Out of the mist a vessel emerged. Less than fifty feet away, a wall of steel, three stories high loomed over the dwarfed yacht. He says he was close enough to read its name.

"What was it?" someone asks.

"I can't read Russian," he laughs.

"Where did you sail from?" a British man asks me, but before I can answer, cannon-fire explodes and the sky is fanned with colours. We all breathe out on cue, a communal voice: *Ahhhh,* we sigh, in appreciation of the fireworks ripping at the night's blackness.

"A toast to All Saint's Day," a voice sings out. Glasses rise in honour of the dead. "Watch out for ghosts and merchant ships!"

Next to me, John and Giles lean back on their chairs, their tanned faces tilted upward towards the flecks of light.

I use the diversion to leave the table and walk to the end of the breakwater where rocks and boulders are strewn like a medieval tower has tumbled into the black water. The sky overhead is perforated with green pinwheels, red shooting stars, and white globes of pulsing light. Yellow spirals with frayed tails gyrate angrily across the sky, and perfect geodesic domes hang like silver Christmas balls. Then, as suddenly as it began, it's over. The gift is snatched away leaving only the moon swinging over Africa.

In the last week I have come to hate the Madeiran moon. It pronounces the passing of time with no modesty for its growing beauty—six nights ago it was a crescent, an airplane skirting its edge, but tonight, it is almost a half. It mocks me with its resemblance to a white hull.

The moon's swelling form, flaunting its false seas, appears innocent while its claw of gravity drags the earth's oceans in and out in dogged rhythms. On beaches around the world, retreating tides parade the lost objects of a mariner's life: a red cap, a tangled web of fishing net, unbound ropes, sand-etched glass, swollen shoes, or, with the errors of navigation, a keel splintered against rock.

I turn away from the night sky and look over the marina. The yachts are quiet and dark except for a few small rectangles of yellow but the restaurants are brightly lit and busy. Chairs and tables have migrated onto the quay. Black-trousered waiters carry heavy-laden trays, squeezing their narrow hips between heads and shoulders. The tourists chatter, drop silverware, clink glasses together. The world looks like a harmless place.

I should go back, back to their fearless laughter. I should ask these recent arrivals, their yachts anchored so safely now, danger a forgotten element—have you heard of *Mugwump*? But I am despairing. Why are you here and not my brother, not Sarah? Hundred of boats cross the same ocean and only one is missing? Where is your humble fear? Why are you not on your knees with gratitude?

I walk past the restaurant, a black shadow pacing a widow's walk.

You can be lost out there, I whisper to the sailors. *And they won't find you.*

I head for the marina phone booth again. It's late to call Canada but I need to talk to someone. As I move past the stone mermaid I remember the nautical saying.

A naked woman before the wind will settle any storm.

This is why shipbuilders put bare-breasted figureheads on ships' prows. According to myth, the sea god, Poseidon, stirs up the oceans and creates storms out of his physical desire. Only a woman's flesh will settle the turbulent god so sailors can pass.

Tonight, the mermaid doesn't look like a protectoress of sailors—a passive figurehead willing to calm a sea god with her nakedness. She is a fury of desire and power. Her flesh unyielding to any force of nature.

Poseidon isn't stirring up the waters, it is her.

I WAKE SIMON UP and say I can't do this.

"What?"

"I'm not a sailor. I was scared today."

"It wasn't really much of a storm. A force six, seven at most."

"If that's true, Simon, then I will never survive a real one."

"You know I can't work in an office, luv," he whispers.

"I know that too."

Simon flings back the sheet and leaves the cabin. I hear him walking on the deck, pausing to strike a match. The scent of tobacco and sea air waft through the open hatch. I stare at the sky. The stars turn.

Ariadne's story doesn't end on Naxos. The goddess Aphrodite, moved by the heroine's grief in finding herself alone, promises her an immortal lover. Dionysus, the bull-god, famous for inciting the passions of mortals, makes Ariadne his wife and takes her to live on Mount Olympus. When Ariadne dies, her faithful husband throws the crown he has given her as a wedding present into the sky. Fixed in the heavens, the constellation *Corona Borealis* is a testament to changed destiny.

ISLAND

The islands are not there, though the clouds
attest to them. All of it, except the sea itself and the
sailors' yearning, is an illusion.

ROBERT FINLEY

FROM THE FRONT SEAT I can see the birds-of-paradise growing out of garbage. Orange and purple blooms, crested like
cockatoos, poise regally on long green necks. At home, florists
sell these flowers as exotics—here they line the roads like
weeds.

"Damn!" Jo shouts. She takes the corner too fast and the
car almost scrapes a low stone wall.

"Good God," Giles groans from the back.

I bat at the bird-of-paradise poking its beak into the car
and then see the bus, engine revving, fuel smoke burning a

grey-blue tail. Jo breaks hard and for a moment we are suspended—trapped between a low parapet that prevents
crumbling asphalt from sliding down the slope and a green,
vibrating wall of metal threatening to push us over the edge. Jo
backs the car up into a bulge in the road. She pulls hard on the
emergency break until the ratcheting sound stops and then
turns her head to look at the two men in the back seat.

"You drive, Giles," she says, flinging the door open to the
smell of diesel.

Giles had been squirming since we left Funchal a half-
hour ago. And although John was the taller one, over six feet
with long thighs angling up like cannon barrels, it was Giles
who was uncomfortable—fingers snapping, hands gripping the
headrest behind my neck, knuckles tapping on the glass as he
hummed an unrecognizable tune. His feet pawed and danced
on the floor mat. Every few minutes he'd stick his head
between the front seats and look at the speedometer.

"Jesus, Jo, it'll take four days to go around the island at this
rate."

"*F*-off, Giles." She had said this just before the green monster bus, its flat nose bearing down on the rented Renault, had
convinced Jo that it would be less stressful to sit in the back.

Giles squeezes out of the car, unfolding his muscular body
like a contortionist realigning the joints. He stretches then gets
into the driver's seat. Sliding his palms over the black steering
wheel, he smiles. He is clearly relieved to be at this helm.

"Sit back and relax folks," Giles says, imitating an
American accent. "You are now in the hands of a master."

It is Jo's turn to groan.

Giles engages the clutch, pushes the gear into first and
brings the car up to fourth before we've made the next corner. With inches to spare and side mirrors almost colliding we

slip past the blur of traffic encroaching into our unmarked lane. The island rises and falls under the car like a great stretching beast.

Now that she's no longer driving, Jo settles into her seat and chats with John. I pick up fragments of the conversation coming from the back seat. Jo is missing her boyfriend who's captaining another boat in Spain. She'll see him next month when she returns *Columban* to the Mediterranean. John's loneliness is different. He's tired of the banking world in London. "Not even thirty and I'm sick of working," he confesses.

"What do you do at home, Giles?" Jo asks, leaning over his shoulder.

Giles finds her eyes in the rear view mirror. "Oh, I play some football," he says, then looks back at the road.

"Why'd you decide to crew?" I ask.

He shrugs. "Bored."

"Is it working?"

"I'm only mildly amused by the idea of sailing 1,500 miles on the Atlantic. Captain's an asshole, food is shit, and of course there's not much sleep. But Madeira is paradise. I like it here."

No one asks me any questions. They already know why I'm here on this island. I don't tell them that I know something of the sea too.

The car trip around the island is Jo's idea.

"What do you think, Cathy? Time to get away from the harbour?" she suggests. "Rent a car? Maybe Giles and John want to join us."

We are sitting up on deck in the bright sunlight. *Columban's* mainsail droops over our heads in loosely tied swags of white canvas. The eighty-foot mast towers like a stripped tree trunk. Jo pours tea while I look across to the town of Funchal—rows of stacked houses are built up the mountainside like the terraced seats of an amphitheatre. I imagine it sliding into the ocean in a torrential rain. Walls and roofs collapsing under the weight of thick mud.

Jo has just finished describing what it's like to be at sea in a storm.

"Sometimes you can hove-to, reef in the sails, turn the boat into the wind and let the sea carry you, but if you're close to a shipping lane or the coastline you can't—you have to keep watch."

Columban rocks. A small wave made by a departing yacht ripples across the water. On the deck two brown puddles encircle our mugs.

"In a rough sea, it's the exhaustion that does you in," says Jo.

During the night, *Columban* creaks and sways like she's riding the waves, and even though I know the yacht is anchored safely in the marina, protected from the Atlantic breakers by a long sea wall, I see her going down, water coming in through the cracked hull.

I cry in my cabin. *What else can I do for them?*

In the dark, David's voice whispers. *We can't be far, Sarah. I smell oranges on the wind.*

THE ROADS OF MADEIRA wind through the land like a wandering cat—over the beaches, across the bluffs, snaking the green hills. Terraces of banana trees are cut into the mountainside. Vineyards step up slopes of eroded ancient volcanoes. Nutty flavoured grapes—sercial, malmsey, tinta negra mole—hang from wooden trellises, their roots deep in the black rich soil. In the hill villages, pink and yellow houses, faded and peeling, sit only a few feet back from the road separated by wrought iron gates. Old women dressed like nuns sit on the steps and peer into the car with obsidian eyes. When the highway dips down to the sea, brightly painted fishing boats dot the shoreline like abandoned sand toys.

For the first time in weeks, I relax. I'm just a tourist, I tell myself, a passenger in a car travelling with strangers. I'm not looking for anyone or anything along these roads. The world rushes by, all new, never seen before, and I am like a child staring through glass.

OUR FAMILY SEDAN ROCKS down the highway. My father steers with one hand, his right arm stretched across the back of the front bench seat. Manitoba slips by the window at fifty miles an hour—hypnotizing pine forests, bright wheat fields, bulrush-edged marshes reflecting a blue sky.

Every summer weekend, we drive to lakes with beaches. Pillows on our laps, Archie comics, a Styrofoam cooler that squeaks when you touch it. In the early years, there were homemade sleeping bags and a green canvas tent. When it rained, our fingers itched to press the sides and bring the water in. Now we have a trailer that sleeps six.

In the summer of 1972, on the long trip from Winnipeg to Banff, my older sister and brother plant themselves next to the car windows and refuse to change places for the two-day drive. Only David and I must move. We take turns sitting between the invisible lines drawn on the backbench by our siblings and the coveted space between our parents. The front seat has the best view as well as under-the-dash vents that suck in asphalt-heated air and blow the scent of oil over our faces. When I'm bored, I turn around to watch my brothers and sister. David is squirming. First, he straddles the driveshaft hump and sticks his legs under the seats, then he leans across my brother's lap and hangs over the highway. His head tosses in the car's wake, hair parting in neat rows like a field of grain.

"The wind has teeth," he shouts, while the road speeds under him, a dizzying blur. My mother reaches for his shirt and pulls him inside.

WE HAVE BROKEN AWAY from the sea.

Giles turns off the highway and we head north into the island's forested mountains. The road narrows and clings to a rock slope wrapped with a low stone wall. The Renault groans as it climbs the steep inclines. Giles has trouble finding the right gear. He tries shifting down for the tight corners of the switchbacks and up for the short straight aways, but either the engine squeals, or it lumbers and almost stalls.

"Fuck it," mutters Giles. He leaves the car in second, pistons pounding under the hood, and takes the corners fast.

Jo is laughing in the back. "I can't watch!"

John is silent, his face hidden from me.

I twist my neck to look up the mountainside to see what's coming down.

"They'll see us before we see them," Giles says to me. A smile widens across his serious, intense face. "Don't worry."

"Male bravado," I say, not very loud.

"We'll be fine. Trust me." He laughs.

A silent agreement is made—there's no time for prudent driving.

Although the island isn't large, only fifty-eight kilometres long and twenty-three kilometres wide, the mountainous terrain is etched with twisting roads balanced on cliff precipices and enough switchbacks to triple the anticipated length of the trip. I keep my eyes focused on the side of the road where a gorge begins to slide away to an unseen valley. Wisps of clouds, thin as cotton gauze, spin up from the treetops like apparitions. Who would find us if we slid quietly over the edge?

The road turns into a one-track lane, descending quickly in a series of short switchbacks. Rain starts to fall, draping the car in long silver ribbons. Pendulous fuchsia blossoms blow across the asphalt, floating like lilies in a black pool. We drive over them, flatten the petals under the tires.

Giles takes a corner fast. I am thrown against his shoulder, my ear sliding down his unshaven cheek. At the next turn, I move back to my side of the car. Clusters of hydrangeas bow their mauve and blue heads at the window. The only way to stop myself from sliding back and forth, is to hold on to the seat with one hand, press the other against the door, and lean with the car when Giles navigates the hairpin turns. But still our bodies collide.

When a thick wall of fog swallows the car, rendering us blind, Giles downshifts abruptly from a halting second gear. His hand slips off the stick and sweeps over my leg. I feel the heat of his skin and wince, shudder.

The rain beats the roof like dropped ball bearings.

I look down at our bodies. It's just a man's hand and the bare thigh of a woman but I see the undressing: buttons slip out of tightly stitched slits, a shirt tail comes free, the blouse falls. Belt buckles, clasps, zippers are opened. Mouths part.

I have forgotten how simple desire can be.

SAM REACHES FOR ME across the bed, not saying a word.

Not, *I'll miss you.* Not, *Be careful.* Not, *I'm sure you'll find out something about David and Sarah.* He doesn't try to make a joke. *Watch out for sailors, you know how you are with sailors.* He doesn't say, *I'm afraid of dying too.* Just his hand on my thigh, weighted like a bag of brown sugar, heavy in its longing.

I roll onto my side, hoping his desire will withdraw and make his abandonment complete. The absences from our family have been lengthening. His treatment for the thyroid cancer is finished, the latest scan shows the overactive cells are gone, but something in my husband has retreated with them and a terrible silence remains. We're abandoned to our fears.

In the darkness, Sam's hand slides up anyway. I lie still under the tense smothering muscle of his body.

"Whatever you do, don't move," he whispers.

Don't move.

I feel myself sinking, going under. Sam grabs me and hangs on, a hand tight around my calf. The sarcasm in his voice becomes clear and I lift my hips, an arm, open my mouth, breathe.

He holds my face, each thumb cantilevered under a cheekbone. His eyes are open in the murky light. The scar at his throat from the banished tumour ruffles like a small wave. He shakes.

This is the moment when a woman disappears inside her skin.

This is when the man soothes his pain.

Our bodies let go and fall. Only a sound hangs—the rattle of air in a throat opening and closing.

Now leave me.

We are quiet, not moving in our pretense of satisfaction. The sheet clings like white paint poured into the hollows of our ribs, our bellies, and the rifts between the thighs.

THE ROAD ENDS IN a glade of chestnut trees draped in lichen thin as lace. Giles slides the car next to a sea of bright ferns waving in the rain. Jo pops the trunk and the four of us crowd together, digging for our jackets. Giles's thigh knocks against mine when he passes me my fleece. I hide the shiver that pounds up my spine by sliding the anorak over my head. I pull the zipper to my neck and shove my cold hands into the pockets. My ribs feel like a cage, guarding emptiness.

There is no light in the forest except for the ghosts of white air we stir with our feet. We walk along a stone path under acacia trees dripping clouds and rain. A satin waterfall pours its liquid silver.

"Be careful here," John says. "It's slippery."

I grip a rock to steady myself but it's too late for the warning. From behind, a hand hits my left shoulder and knocks me off balance. My heels slip on the wet stones and I slide backwards, falling against something solid.

Giles either catches me or is clinging to save himself.

"Sorry," he says. "Couldn't stop myself."

His hands grip my shoulders, burn through the jacket.

"Did I hurt you?"

My skin is pulling away from bone and muscle. Something has a hold of every tiny hair on my arms and legs and is tugging hard.

Don't move, I want to say to him. Leave your hands. Press harder. Hold me.

But I step away.

Out in the open, away from the matted cover of twisted trees, I stand in the falling rain with closed eyes.

I cannot collapse here. There are lives to hold together. My children. Sam. David. And Sarah. I am here to find their missing bodies, not my own.

We continue along the path, slipping and sliding. Our feet leave oval hollows in puddles of soft moss. We grip tree roots, boulders, each other for balance.

I deliberately touch them. A casual grip of John's arm. Fingertips on Jo's back. I squeeze between John and Giles when we stop to toss stones into the creek.

Touching has become as necessary as breathing. Like a dance, I roll my body to quiet the slow burn under my skin.

Jo points out a clump of calla lilies growing on top of a rock wall. The blooms are filled with rain like porcelain teacups left outside. I reach for one of the white funnels.

If I unravel, this island will sink.

If I speak, loneliness will flow out of me, I will seek love with another sailor, and we will all drown.

The petals close around me, hold me in their cool wax.

Can we forgive our unbidden desires?

THERE IS A MOOR IN Madeira, a deserted wind-swept plateau similar to a Scottish heath—a flat broad heart in the middle of the island.

The car climbs out of the lush wet forest and we come upon a barren scene: a treeless plain, air coloured grey and tan—soft as the hide of a deer. It's like the sky has come down to us, a great woolen blanket shaken and lowered.

In the dim light, I can imagine the birthing of this island. Molten rock pushed out of the sea, fire spilling into salted steam, and then the cooling—epochs of time passing before the brute molecules spin into life, and the world's first dream is made alive.

The car doors open to a quiet world. The rain has stopped pitting the roof. The only sound is our footsteps, splintered shale breaking like shells as we disappear in the enveloping mist.

Jo drifts into the fog and fades, the air wrapping her in a flaxen gown. Giles is swept away as if a painter's broad strokes are returning him to the background of a canvas. John's body is altered into a khaki-clad figure moving through smoke.

I look at my hand: it floats, fingers point at something in the distance—a man, or is it a stag held in absolute stillness, the animal quickened to danger?

When did we see the sky last? my brother whispers.

Was it only yesterday that the rain came, pulling down the clouds, hiding us from the world? Was that the first crack, the splinter, the swelling? Is that when she heaved, spine giving way, the sea rushing in to fill up the spaces?

Oh, Sarah. I remember the soft row of moons down your back.

I remember when we rolled under a blue sky, our skin the same colour as Australian sand.

Soon it will be the same as sea, Sarah.

Is that when the lovemaking is over?

"Give me your hand, Cathy." Giles appears out of thin air and reaches through the mist. "There's a steep bank, here."

I look at his upturned palm, wide like a prairie field. I imagine lying down in it, my skin pressing into warm soil, rolling under tall grass, wheat, the heavy-headed barley curled in the wind on a summer day. My flesh becoming the earth's flesh.

I take a breath to steady myself. The air is thick like the sky is falling. The soft weight of velvet nudges me closer to the edge.

"Come this way," Giles says. His hand touches my back.

We cross the moor, our calves splattered with red earth.

"You know, I think fog's worse than rain," Jo says. "It's suffocating."

The scent of sea air enters the car and tugs at my sleepiness. I open my eyes and see a small town below us. Porto Moniz. The most northerly point of the island. Giles rolls down the window and sweeps his arm through the air. He finds the strains of a Lennon/McCartney song and beats a rhythm on the roof.

"*Here comes the sun*, finally," says John.

Jo smiles, the sky caught in her eyes. "That weather was really getting to me."

ON THE TERRACE OF the Orca Hotel, Giles and I sit at a table with four empty beer bottles. John and Jo have gone wandering into the small white town that cooks in the hot sun. Giles is finishing a second beer. I'm staring at the sea pool below us.

I watch a man and a woman step into the water and follow the white submerged sidewalk. When they get to the end of the walkway they propel themselves forward, swimming over the sandy floor and around the rocks. The man swims faster than the woman, the practiced stroke of a front crawl curving over his head. When he reaches the pool's edge, the waves are cascading and retreating in white foam. He leans on the concrete wall, holding it while the surf pushes at his shoulders, and calls to the woman. A language of disparate sounds echoes in the air. She answers him with one word and swims away, gliding, flesh rippling under the surface. She returns to the underwater sidewalk where she can touch. The man calls to her again, his voice louder.

"What do you suppose he's saying to her?" I ask Giles.

"Get your ass over here or I'll come and drag it back myself."

"He's got to be saying more than that. He's been yelling for over a minute."

"Maybe he's a poet, comparing her lovely body to a seal's."
Giles grins.

When the woman ignores him, the man pushes up and
swings his tanned legs onto the two-foot-wide barrier that
keeps the sea back. He stands up. Water rushes over his calves.
He calls to her again and this time she turns around and sees
him with his arms stretched out in preparation for a dive.

"Maybe he's saying, *Look, I can walk on water*," I say.

Now the woman is angry and she begins her own tirade,
spitting words into the air while she raises her arms in disgust.

"You know, Giles, if the waves pull him back he'll drown
on the other side."

"He won't fall."

"How do you know?"

"He won't fall."

Giles is right. The sea pushes him up into the air before he
arcs, hands splitting the water. He glides along the bottom and
comes up under the woman, his arms lifting her legs. She
laughs. He presses his mouth against her ear and she laughs
some more. The lovers leave the pool, spread striped beach towels on the cement platform and lay close to each other. The
man trails his hand in the water, small waves lapping at his wrist.

The afternoon sun drives the other tourists inside to the air-
conditioned restaurant. Giles and I watch the ocean, waves
slamming into pillars of basalt—a scattered army of stone
caught in the surf. Funnels of white spray shoot upward like
geysers and rain down.

"Have you heard anything?" Giles asks. He peels back the
corner of a beer label.

"About my brother and Sarah?"

"Yeah."

I shake my head.

He scratches at the word *Coral*. The paper lifts in long strips. "What does the coastguard say?"

"Not much. According to them, a jury-rigged yacht or a life raft would be at the whim of the winds and sea currents."

Giles nods. "The trades are steady. They blow from the north, all the way down the Iberian coastline. Some say once you're past Finisterre, you're home free."

They'll be found, I want him to say. Declaring with absolute confidence that David and Sarah will be all right, like the man in the pool who wasn't pulled into the open sea. But Giles turns away and looks west. His eyes pull in a deep colour from the horizon line. A breeze flattens the white t-shirt against his chest.

"We were lucky," he says. "We caught the wind coming out of Lisbon. It blew us right here."

A dark lizard climbs over the terrace wall, notices our presence and stops mid-motion. Reptilian skin bursts into rows of tiny flames. The glass eyes stare. We stare back, waiting for the lizard to move. Giles sweeps his hand through the air, a gesture similar to passing a hand in front of someone's eyes when we think they are lost to this world. The shadow crosses back and forth over the S-shaped body and tail. The lizard doesn't notice. He clings upside down.

"My brother likes wind," I say to Giles. "He tried hang-gliding about ten years ago. He used to go to this place called Grand Beach, about an hour from where we grew up. He'd run along the tops of the sand dunes. He was always hoping an off-shore wind would lift him up." I see him kicking up the soft white sand, trying to step onto air with yellow wings. "But the highest he ever flew was when he tied the glider to the back of a friend's car and they drove the road between the beach town and the campground. Eventually the Mounties saw the fool flying fifty feet over the road and made him stop."

Giles laughs. "Well, he sounds like a fun guy. I tried bungee jumping once. Surprisingly, it wasn't like falling. It was a leap into air with the belief that something will catch you and pull you back."

"Faith in elastic rubber."

"Faith in something."

Giles stretches his arm across the table. He spreads his palm flat on the metal surface. I hold back my desire to touch his hand.

"It's hard to believe I sailed this ocean just two days ago," he says quietly. "It seems larger from here."

I LEAVE THE TABLE and go in search of Jo and John but instead find a sheltered cove with a narrow pebbled shoreline. Rows of knitted waves break at my feet. A scuba diver, rubber black like a seal, and carrying only a single tank, slips into the water from the edge of a pier. The sea folds over him, leaving a scar of white foam. Air bubbles rise in a furious cluster. The tip of a spear gun pierces the surface and then he is gone.

I wonder how deep the man will go.

Will he dare to leave this shallow bay, venturing out to where the sea is dark, and the large ocean currents sweep along the island? It's the Canary Current out there. A river over half a kilometre deep.

The North Atlantic is both sea and river, an eternal clockwise circle of water. Dragged along by the wind, the Gulf Stream travels up the coast of the U.S. until the edge of the Grand Banks forces it east. At the Azores archipelago, a southern branch splits off and the Canary Current heads south and moves slowly past this island. When the current reaches the

Cape Verde Islands, a third of the way down the coast of Africa, it flows west with a new name, the North Equatorial Current. The loop is now closed and the river returns to the Caribbean.

How long does it take for these waters to circle the North Atlantic? Six months? A year? Where were we when they rushed through the Straits of Florida, pulled north by the wind?

I AM MAKING HALLOWEEN costumes—a hippie girl, Davy Crockett, a sheep.

Sam is coming home late from work, tugging at his shirt collar. "The dry cleaners are shrinking my shirts," he complains.

David has a night job cooking sausages and chips at the Sussex Brewery in Emsworth. After his shift he crosses a two-hundred-year-old wooden floor, thick with sawdust, and slides up to the bar for a quick beer. Some nights he drives to the Tarquin Yacht Harbour before continuing home to Sarah.

He writes to me about *Mugwump* on blue translucent air-mail paper: *She's beautiful and every time I leave her I just have to turn around and have one last look. No, Sarah's not getting jealous, she's in love too!*

A year ago, their voyage is still a dream.

Fingers tap on my back and release a shiver up my spine.

"There you are. We've been looking for you."

Giles crouches down beside me. His arms rest across tanned muscular thighs. The watch on his wrist burns silver in the sunlight. How long have I sat here, waiting for the glossy head of the diver to re-emerge?

"We've got to go now," Giles says. "There's an island to cross before dark."

I know where we must go. Follow the cracked edge of northern Madeira, keep the sea on our left, a blue solemn plain, then turn inland and cross the high forests of the Montado. But then where? A slide down the mountain to Funchal, back to the marina and its ghosts? A descent into *Columban's* hull with Giles's hand pressing on the small of my back? And there shall I offer what I have, whatever remains of me—this despair masked as desire, this yearning to be broken open and saved?

I take out the turtle rock I've been carrying and put it into the water. A small wave rolls over the top, darkening the green colour. I throw it as far as I can, whispering, *Swim.*

GILES CARVES THE CORNERS and tunnels of the North Coast Road like he's Villeneuve on the Monaco circuit. Deep in the seat, left hand fused to the steering wheel, right fist driving the gearshift in a tight *H* pattern. His thigh, knee, and ankle are fluid with the clutch—depressing then releasing in quick opposite motions to the accelerator. I hold my breath.

We fly the narrow corniche defiantly, the road aimed at sky, an invisible thread pulling us into air. The single lane twists and hangs over the ocean, a two-foot parapet marking its edge. My eyes seek the fall—a crumbling cliff, a five-hundred-foot plunge to the bursting surf roiling on rocks below.

At each blind corner, Giles honks and Jo yelps, an amusement-ride shriek.

"We should have one of those vintage trumpet horns," John laughs. "Ah-oogah!"

Every few hundred metres we enter an unlit tunnel, blinded by sudden blackness—falling, a deep hole, throats thickening—until our pupils widen, search the darkness, and chase the car's two beams of light glancing off blasted rock bright as shoe polish. Water trickles through cracks, echoes in the cavern. The air is cement cool. The hair on our arms stands on end.

"Let's go dancing tonight," Jo says, right before a waterfall, straying off its original course, explodes onto the car hood and floods the windshield like a breaking wave. We duck instinctively while Giles slams clutch and brake, pulls the stick back and flips on the wipers.

"Thrilling," Jo murmurs. She leans forward between Giles and I. "So? Dancing? There's a club down by the docks that's supposed to be not too bad."

The road straightens. The engine whine changes to a purr.

Dancing. Bodies circling bodies. Hands dragging across hips. Sweat. Holding. There would be holding.

Cliff walls sweep by the glass—a blur of reptilian vines.

I could pour like liquid.

I could forget.

THE HIGHWAY FOLLOWS THE coastline like a long dark ribbon trimming a skirt hem. I stare out the window at deserted scenes: faded fishing boats tilting against rocks, the spilled cradles left to rot in the surf; a broken church, hanging on a cliff, tombstones and crosses leaning away from the wind; old men watching the sea, peeling paint falling into grey hair. Even the sea is a forgotten blue dress washed up on shore.

The sun is just setting as Giles turns the car into the mountains. The storm clouds, piled along the horizon, follow us inland. We drive past farmhouses balanced on terraced slopes, their faded shutters closed until morning. Dusk falls like ash over the fruit trees—bananas, grapefruits, and pears hang in their muted waxed flesh. Overhead, a cold pewter sky descends.

When the rain hits, Giles doesn't slow down. The car climbs, twisting through the switchbacks, engine whining.

Water is dragged back and forth across the windshield. Leaves catch in the thrashing blades.

"Everyone, stop breathing," Giles demands. He wipes away the condensation with his open palm but the fog returns, a hidden mouth pressed up to the glass.

I lean my head against the door and look through the window. There's too much water. Have we fallen into the ocean? At a switchback, a shearing crosswind slams against the car. I hear rigging hammering a mast.

I see her in the glass. Perched on top of a crest-ripped wave for a brief, tottering moment, *Mugwump* floats. She is beautiful. Her deck glows red under a beam of moonlight. Her sails, torn into ribbons, fly like kite strings across a sky. The long narrow hull lifts into air until she resembles a breaching whale, the black keel arching in flight.

She has forgotten she is a boat meant for water.

Where are you?
Here.
Where?
In the air. I'm the wind.
Then I will be the wind too. Circling the earth. Eroding land, flattening hills, smoothing the peaks of mountains over time. Shores will fall away, crumble and fill in the sea. If I were the wind, I'd travel the world in one breath and carry sailors home.
When you are the wind there is no home.

Giles's hand grips my knee and gives it a small shake.

"You all right?"

I turn to his face, pale in the headlights of a passing car, the profile—one I've known forever—the brow, the nose, a cleft in the chin, a hero's image stamped on a coin a thousand years ago.

If I were the wind, I wouldn't be afraid of destruction or desire.

I'd have *him*.

Two moons bright as searchlights drop out of darkness in the middle of the road.

The car breaks hard.

Giles flings his arm across my chest, holds me against the seat as we slide into the light.

My heart collides with bone.

Oh, God. A voice from behind.

Round, glowing orbs hover. Faces are bleached white.

We shut our eyes and wait for the sound.

When we fling open the car doors, the scent of pine hits first, then a trace of eucalyptus, the gelatinous balm for heaving chests.

"I can't breathe," I tell Jo.

"No shit," she answers, bending over.

"Fucking close, Giles," says John.

"The corner was blind," shouts Giles. He picks up a rock from the side of the road and pitches it into the forest. "The bus didn't even know we were there."

But no one knows where we are. It's easy to be lost, not seen in this world.

I feel Giles's hand on my shoulder. "We're OK," he says.

Yes, I breathe.

I lean into him. A button, a cool slice of shell presses into my cheek.

This day has been a dream. A damp and green circumnavigation of an island. And like the lily, calling me to slip my hand into its narrow bloom, it is a reminder that I am still alive.

The button on Giles's shirt grows hot, burns like a small branding iron on my flesh. This island will leave a scar.

SINKING

The sea severs not only lands,
but also selves.

WALLACE STEVENS

COLUMBAN DRAWS A LOT of attention in the Funchal Marina.
Tourists, locals and sailors saunter by for a view of the
wide black deck, the looming masts, and the row of round
portholes. When they get close to her, they smile, tilt their
heads back and guess the height of the tallest spar. Viewing the
ship up close seems to please them, perhaps igniting the memory of a seafaring book they read as a child. But tonight's
crowd gathered at *Columban's* mooring is different. Instead of
curious, the people are solemn. Some are crouching down, fingertips grazing the quay, their heads bowed as if the boat is a
coffin lowering into the earth.

Jo sees the crowd first and breaks into a run. John, Giles, and I follow her, dodging couples and families out for an after-dinner stroll. When we reach the throng we push our way to the front, hands pressing against backs and shoulders, strangers parting to let us through.

At first I don't understand why the boat is so far below us. At eight this morning, I stepped easily across the gangway from the deck to the quay, but now, thirteen hours later, I cannot see how we will be able to board—*Columban* is at least seven or eight feet lower. Has the sea receded? A tide so low that the ship will bottom out in the harbour, its keel a knife in the mud? And why are her masts still?

Jo jumps down. Her hair flies behind like a blond cape. John and Giles follow with easy bounds.

I hear the owner of the yacht tied next to *Columban,* say to Jo, "I'm glad you're back. I didn't know what to do but loosen the mooring lines."

"Cathy, come on!" A man's voice from below calls to me.

I look down. Seven feet below is a two-foot span of water between the boat and the cement wall of the quay. Black oily water slops along the hull like the backs of seals.

"I can't jump, Giles."

"Sure you can. It's not as far as you think."

I toss my sandals onto the deck, the metal buckles ringing against a winch, and then fling my bag towards Giles. I bend my knees to spring forward but I am glued to the cement.

"Here, use the mooring line. Walk on it," Giles says. He takes a step towards me, one leg balancing on the gunnels.

I slip my foot onto the rope, test the tautness, and start to inch forward. "Now take my hand, and I'll hold on to you," he says. A man standing behind me on the quay kneels down and offers his hand for balance. I shuffle the few steps between the two men, my toes curling over the twisted line, until Giles grips my forearm and guides me onto the deck.

"There," he says. "That wasn't so bad."

His hand draws away slowly, a brief lingering of fingertips pressed into flesh. I feel its absence like a sore bruise.

Giles puts a yellow pail into my hand and disappears into the darkness of the hull.

I walk across the deck. *Columban* is eerily quiet. She does- n't creak. She doesn't moan. Like an old woman with a silent chest, *Columban* is no longer breathing.

She is sinking.

In the salon, the water is already up to the third rung of the companionway—two-and-a-half feet of liquid, black and vis- cous as molasses. The seawater laps at the lower cupboards like black tongues reeking of diesel.

The yellow pail will save this?

"The pump couldn't keep up with it," Jo says, standing in water up to her thighs.

I remember the sound we had woken to this morning—a high-pitched whining, an urging, vibrating alarm. Jo thought a sensor was detecting water but the bilge was dry. We had eggs for breakfast while the ringing continued. When Giles and John arrived the alarm was intermittent. And then finally it went silent. Jo thought it might be a short, some faulty wiring. There was no water in the hull when we left *Columban* this morning. The sea must have leaked in slowly.

A conga line is formed, first with Giles, John, Jo and I, and then crew from other boats, and then bystanders who jump onto the deck. Pails of water are carried hand over hand and dumped over the side.

"The boat is huge, Giles. It'll take days at this rate."

He slops water on my feet. "I heard Jo say someone's trying to locate a pump."

I take a pail from John's hand and pass it to Giles. Our fingers touch. We are cold and wet.

"I guess this means we're not going dancing," John says.

I pass the pails from left to right, trying to find a rhythm that eases the work and silences my imagination. Last night I had dreamed that *Columban* was going down. A crack slit open the hull. The sea found a way in. But it was a thought, just an imagined fear. Despair can't make holes in matter, or can it?

Boats are designed to float, a coastguard officer had once assured me. Not sink in quiet marinas because someone has a nightmare. "I think I'm bad luck," I say to Giles but he doesn't hear me.

I avoid Jo's eyes as she moves around the boat, but I watch her. After three hours, and with only inches of water removed, she still shows no frustration. She checks the mooring, lugs water, she even laughs at the scene of twenty people passing pails. There is no strain on her face or in her body yet she seems to be aware of *Columban's* stress. She crosses the deck quickly but with light steps, purposeful in her movements like a ballroom dancer who faces one way but slides in the opposite direction.

I wonder what Sarah is like on her boat. I imagine her steps light and quick too. Knees slightly bent, her body slipping under the boom. Does she respond to *Mugwump* out of instinct? The steady balancing of all the forces present. When she feels doubt does it lead to decision or inertia?

"You're walking too fast," David calls after Sarah.

"I'm fine," she says, and she throws her arms above her head. She skips along the Carsaig Arches trail, carved into a steep slope that hangs over the ocean. Boulders the size of trucks litter the Mull shoreline. Waves break on the rocks and shatter into tall rooster tails.

"Be careful," he urges. He crouches down, his fingertips clutching at the sharp edges of a rock face.

"Are you afraid of heights, David?" I ask.

"No. I just get vertigo sometimes."

"I didn't know that about you."

"I only get it in extreme conditions. Like here. Sarah, slow down!"

"Oh, David," she laughs lightly, but doesn't change her pace. She's a mountain goat and her balance is perfect.

"Do you get dizzy looking up or down?" I ask.

David arches his neck and looks up the cliffside. A bird sweeps down from the ridge.

"Both. Definitely both. You go ahead, Cath. I can do this. I just have to go slow."

"OK."

I take off down the path, following Sarah. I glance back when the slope curves around to the right. My brother is clinging with both hands and not moving. He looks afraid. As if at any moment he'll slide away.

Sometime after midnight, a fire truck rumbles along the narrow quay, horn blaring, uniformed men hanging off its sides. It stops in front of *Columban*. A yellow spinning strobe flashes like lightning strikes. Five men walk to the quay's edge, stand in a row, and stare down at the boat. There is much pointing and upturned palms while their heads shake back and forth. Two of them jump down and consult with Jo. She nods her head. A hose is dropped over the side and lowered into the hull. The pump on the truck begins to draw the water out. A second hose dumps it back into the harbour.

We watch from the stern, empty hands, wet shoes. Jo grins as the water slides through the fabric-wrapped hose snaked across the deck. In only half-an-hour, *Columban* starts to shudder and we feel her lifting. She groans like a whale rising to the surface. *Saved.*

When the firemen pull the hose back, we go below deck to see what's ruined. I run a hand over a bulkhead. It is cool, oily, like the skin of a sea creature. The floor is slippery too. Under the table, a sodden magazine curls like a nautilus shell around the centre post. In a corner, a glass rolls slowly back and forth. There is no obvious damage here but I feel sick to my stomach. Where is the crack that let the water in?

"John, let's go see if someone will sell us a bottle of something," Jo says. Twenty minutes later she swings into the galley, *Beefeater* in hand, and a sweeping smile across her face. She is the triumphant piratess back from the plunder.

The gin lasts until five.

"SLOW DOWN!"

I wake to damp air and the sound of a man's voice travelling through the open hatch above my cabin. *Slow down.*

I close my eyes against a piercing shaft of sunlight and go back to my dream.

David and I are running in the forest along King's Drive in the opposite direction from the old German fort. The fort is really just the stone foundation of an abandoned house, but we imagine it as a former stronghold. *It was bombed in the Second World War,* we invent. That accounts for the collapsed roof and blown-out windows and doors. Old shirts, half buried in the rubble, are proof there were victims.

"Are we running from the Germans?" David asks, when we stop to take a breath.

"Worse. Their ghosts."

"What happens if they catch us?"

"No one has lived to tell."

"Oh."

"Okay, now. Let's sprint to that next group of trees. We'll hide behind them." I take off. I am a good runner.

"Don't go so fast! Wait for me!" he shouts.

I turn around. David's hair has burst into flame. The sun has directed its beam on him. The Germans will find him easily now.

I swing my legs over the edge of the bunk and press my feet onto clammy wooden floorboards. The cabin is a mess. Sheets of wet paper are balled and torn. Blurred ink, words spilling off the pages. I can see my leather sandals, one in each corner of the cabin. They are swollen and dark.

I open the cabin door and knock a cup across the floor. In the salon my foot hits a stainless steel knife and sends it spinning like a compass.

Columban smells bad this morning. Really bad. Like seaweed and diesel and fish heads. Like last night's near disaster.

"It's a beautiful day," John says when I appear on the lowest rung of the companionway.

"A little too much beauty, I think." My head feels like pulp.

"We came to say goodbye and to return the zodiac," he says. I look towards the stern of the boat and see Giles tying up a second inflatable. "We're leaving this morning. Captain says the weather's good and we'll catch a trade south. Wind on our backs all the way to Tenerife."

Jo climbs up the steps behind me, a hand pressed to her forehead. "Well, it's good to know you weren't lost out there, motoring around, looking for your ship in the dark. It was pretty foggy."

"Like soup," John says.

"It was?" Giles asks.

Their departure from *Columban* this morning had been drawn-out, like the long bridge game that had to be abandoned when John remembered an early duty shift. Giles had drunkenly argued with him.

"GILES, WE GOTTA GO," says John. "It's after five and the captain'll have a shit."

"Fuck the captain. Two hearts."

"Two spades," I answer. "I think." The cards are swimming in my hands.

"Giles, our shift started 15 minutes ago."

"We're celebrating. Remember, John? The boat almost sank? Have another drink and relax." Giles turns to me. "Four hearts."

I haven't got a single heart but my spades are long—Jack to Ace and some numbers. Someone probably forgot to shuffle the deck from the last hand.

"I hope you've got plenty of hearts, Giles, to justify a four bid."

"Enough for two," he says to me, smiling. "We'll be fine."

"I'm leaving, Giles," says John. "Are you coming?"

Giles pitches his cards across the table. "First decent hand all night."

Jo lets them borrow *Columban's* zodiac.

"Which way is up?" Giles asks, rolling about like a seal in the grey dawn. His flesh squeals as he falls against the black rubber pontoons.

It takes John ten tries to start the motor. Arm pulling. Arm pulling. *Put.* Pulling. *Put put put.* John salutes with his left hand. Throttles with the right.

"You'll capsize us with your swaying, mate," he says putting a foot on Giles. Jo and I watch them leave, the small inflatable retreating into fog.

"I hope you hear something about your brother soon," John says.

"Thank you."

I hug Giles, too, my cheek grazing his own. "It's been nice to meet you," I say. The faint scent of pine floats at his throat. I wait for the resurgence of desire to wash over me but there is nothing. The storm of longing that swept under my skin has blown away. *Columban's* near sinking brought me back to reality.

"I hope *Columban's* okay," Giles says to Jo putting his arm around her.

John climbs into the dinghy but Giles turns around, comes back and kisses me. The gesture is tender but uncertain. Our bodies are long in their retreat.

Giles steps into the grey zodiac. He stands, his arms spread wide. He smiles, as if to say, *See, I won't fall.*

"Where've you been?"

Sam's voice shouts at me from the bottom of a well.

"You haven't called in four days!"

My head hurts. My chest tightens.

"There's been a lot going on here, Sam."

"Some news? Did you find something?" The edge in his voice softens.

I don't know how to tell him that it's all been a waste of time.

"Are the children all right?" I ask.

"I can't hear you very well. Just a second. I'll get a different phone."

The receiver rattles on the counter.

"Mommy?"

"Tegan, you can talk to Mommy in a minute," Sam interrupts. "Hang up the phone now."

"Mommy?"

"Victoria, hang up the phone in the kitchen," Sam yells.

"Hi, Mom. Bye, Mom." *Click.*

"OK. Now what were you saying?"

"I've booked my flight. I arrive Tuesday."

"That's good. It's time to come home."

"I know." I close my eyes.

My legs are shaking. Something is beginning where we cannot see it.

"You know you did everything you could."

Somewhere there are islands being born—an archipelago rolling its curved back, brushstrokes of new white sand drying in the sun.

"I did nothing for them. I discovered nothing." All I've done is stir up my own discontent. The beauty of this landscape, the memories of Simon, the indulgences of my imagination have created a desperate longing. I am going home emptier than when I arrived. "You were right, Sam. I came too late."

My mouth is dry as if a lizard's tail is whipping across my teeth. I lick my lips and taste salt. I taste fish, seaweed, I bite down and crunch shells. When I try to swallow my throat fills with sand. An encroaching desert, dark and silent, is choking me.

I have made a mistake.

I was wrong about David's secret. It has harmed him and Sarah.

David thought he was taking the easy route: unwilling to bear the judgments of his family he kept his voyage a secret. And I had laughed. We were like a couple of immature teenagers, lying about where we were going on a Friday night.

Of course he should have told our parents. I should have told our parents. They deserved the truth. They were left in the dark for so long, it was cruel.

Kerry should have been one of the first to know. Although my two brothers have radically different lives, they have a bond—a love and a skill with all things mechanical. Kerry might have bought David an EPIRB.

And Diane? That was probably David's biggest mistake. His eldest sister, had she known, would have tracked *Mugwump's* voyage daily. She would have been in contact with the coast-guard after ten days at sea. She would never have forgotten that he was on the ocean. For a month.

David told the wrong sister.

I call Diane. The phone rings but no one picks up. The operator tells me to try again later.

I replace the receiver and walk down to the mermaid. I've never paid any attention to the graffiti before. *I LOVE YOU* is scratched across the left flank of her tail. A cross is cut into the stone above the words *NIRVANA*. Today, the mermaid looks benevolent instead of angry. Her hands are not raised in fury but turned upward in gratitude. Those who look upon her body know they have arrived safely.

I walk through the marina, watching the masts sway in the afternoon breeze. After a week in this harbour they still look like metronomes counting out time. In my mind, I see a wooden pyramid open on a piano lid. The pendulum swings. A panel-walled basement fills with dust motes and Beethoven.

DIANE ASKS ME TO turn the pages but I can't stand to sit still for so long.

She stays at the piano, the two-hundred-dollar upright that my father stripped and varnished—except for the swivel seat where he left the chipped grey paint as a reminder of a former incarnation. On a dare, David sneaks across the linoleum tile, hits the piano keys with a splayed hand and runs away. *Fur Elise* continues, the trills barely broken by David's sudden chord. I prompt him to do it again and he gets to the middle of the room as Diane begins the second part of the piece. The music is now agitated, as is the pianist who is slamming the keys. When David reaches her shoulder, Diane's vibrating left hand scares him off and he runs away screaming.

David and I run up the stairs, laughing.

Our sister keeps playing.

I return to *Columban* along the breakwater wall. A hundred white birds are perched on its edge. Black heads and beaks dart nervously. Their dark forked tails remind me of magpies. As I approach, the flock quiets and then falls away like a wind has blown them off the edge. The birds scatter towards the open sea, flying to the four directions—pinholes in a blue sky, crying.

I climb up on the sea wall and look over the marina.

A white-hulled yacht is leaving, motoring to clear the harbour before raising the sails. I can just read the name as it passes by: *Annie-Belle*.

"Hope the captain tossed his hat overboard," a man shouts up to me.

"Why?"

"It appeases the wind gods. And you don't want to get on their bad side."

A soft breeze is coming off the water. The sky is cloud free. It looks like it might be a calm night whether a hat was tossed or not. The crew should have stars and the moon until morning. But then I remember that the harbour is on the south side of the island, sheltered from the prevailing north winds. Conditions in the open sea will be different.

I turn back to the man but he's gone. My eye searches the quay. There is no one around. Half the yachts have left and the boats that remain are bare. It's like the marina has emptied out and the hulls are deserted shells.

"The exodus has begun," Jo explains when I ask her why the marina is so quiet. "The sailors are heading south. Some will winter on the Canary Islands or Cape Verde. Others will push on to the Caribbean. The cross-Atlantic races will begin soon. The ARC Race from Gran Canaria, the Tradewind Race from Tenerife. In ten days, the Funchal Marina will seem like a ghost town. Even I'll be gone."

Then there'll be no one left to keep an eye out for *Mugwump*.

I WAIT IN A hallway in the Customs House. An officer ducks his head into the port captain's office. The man gestures towards me as if to say, *She's here again. Fourth time this week*. I imagine Mr. Aragão behind his desk, leaning back, pressing his fingers along his scalp. A thick gold ring passes through his hair, glinting against the black. What will he say this time? How many ways can he offer hopeful scenarios?

"Come in," Mr. Aragão says, coming to the door.

"Thank you for seeing me. I know we didn't have an appointment."

"You are welcome at any time. How are you?"

"I've a bit of a headache."

"Too much *vinho da roda*?"

"Wine of the round voyage," I translate. The phrase refers to the seventeenth century shipping practice of carrying barrels of wine as ballast. Crossing the equator twice with it ensured perfect aging. "Actually, it was a late night. And it was gin. Did you hear about *Columban*?"

"Yes. When boats start sinking in the marina, I hear about it. Do they know why?"

"Jo thinks it was a faulty seal." In my mind I see the small crack forming, my despair splitting a rubber ring, the sea finding a way to me.

"How is the ship?"

"A bit of a mess. The engine was immersed. That can't be good. But, all in all, I guess it's okay."

"A strange thing," says the port captain. "Sinking in a marina. But with boats, anything can happen."

The room is warm. The fan spins noisily above our heads, making small currents of humid air. The file folder on my lap slips to the floor. Photographs, faxes, and posters slide under the desk.

Mr. Aragão comes around and kneels down beside me. "I'm sorry," he says, gathering the paper into his hands. "You've come such a long way to find your brother and I've been little help."

"But you have helped. That's why I've come by. To thank you before I go home."

He passes me the spilled sheets. "I'm sorry about Falmouth. So much time has passed. They did not think another broadcast would help."

"I know."

"Please, sit down, again. I have something to show you."

He remains standing while he slides two sheets of paper

towards me. The fan casts grey slivers of shadow across his hands.

"What's this?" I ask.

"It's a fax from the Portugal Institute of Meteorology."

At the top is typed:

Meteorological information for 1–10 September 1995 for the Atlantic side involving a possible trip from the South of Ireland to the island of Madeira.

"Did Falmouth send it?"

"No, I requested it. These are the weather **conditions** for the region of the North Atlantic that *Mugwump* was attempting to cross."

I continue to read.

From September 1 to September 5, winds ranged from force 3 to force 7 with wave heights reaching 4 metres. On September 6, a deep depression situated southwest of Ireland moved east with a cold front of strong intensity. West winds reached force 7 with squalls of 50 knots.

"Do you understand the Beaufort Scale?" he asks.

"I've forgotten."

He sits down slowly, glancing at an open binder on the desk. "There are thirteen categories describing wind strength at sea. For example, force three is a gentle breeze. Force seven is a near gale with winds up to sixty kilometres per hour. The Beaufort Scale also describes the sea's appearance. Wave height. Visibility. Changes in the way crests break."

I look back down at the report.

On September 7, the deep depression is between the south of Ireland and the Finisterre Cape in northern Spain. Winds from the west/northwest of force 10 to 12 on the Beaufort Scale with squalls of 80 knots.

"Force ten?" I ask.

"Force ten and eleven are considered violent storms. Winds of over ninety kilometres per hour. Wave heights can reach fourteen metres." He pauses. He doesn't look at my eyes but stares at the paper in my hand. "With winds of over one hundred and twenty kilometres, force twelve is called a hurricane."

The ceiling fan clicks above my head.

There is always hope, we had declared in this heavy air.

My voice trembles. "Falmouth told me three weeks ago that the weather wasn't unusual for this region of the North Atlantic. I was told they were *normal* equinox storms." I stare at the fax, a sickly grey sheen. "I've made a mistake. I thought *normal* meant *not dangerous*."

The port captain leans forward over the desk, clasps his small hands together and drops his head. "What is there to say about storms...?"

ICARUS AND HIS SISTER

The boy, his heart, aspiring to the sky,
And soared aloft: through nearness to the sun
The wax, that bound the wings, began to run;
The fastenings flew: he flapped bare arms in air,

OVID

THE WIND IS HERE and gone like a lost child.

He was right beside me a moment ago, mothers wail and, of course, they are right. Children fade into crowds, turn corners in stores, run into water not knowing its depths. They are known to stay hidden even when adults call their names.

Parents warn their children not to stray. *Stay where I can see you*, they insist, because they understand that the young have a tendency to wander. Even Daedalus warned his son, *Don't fly too close to the sun, Icarus.* But he put wings on the boy. What did he expect? Could he not imagine that his son wouldn't listen, or that a fiery star would draw the boy higher and higher with its promise of beauty? But Daedalus never saw the inevitable— melted wings spiralling into the sea. The craftsman and inventor didn't predict that the twists and turns of his famous labyrinth would one day be repeated by a body falling through the sky, the flailing limbs of his own son.

What remained for Daedalus after the sea opened and swallowed his Icarus?

What remains for me?

A deafening silence. And a memory.

We wait with snow.

The storm begins with snowflakes—floating like shaken feathers from a torn pillow. By mid-morning, they are falling in clumps, splattering cars, sidewalks, and mailboxes.

"It's like bird poop," I say to David.

We plead to go outside but the answer is no. You won't be able see an inch in front of your faces, our mother claims. So, we wait. We wait in front of the living room window watching snowflakes hit the glass like mud from a spinning tire. And we listen to the wind.

Sometimes we catch a glimpse of thin tree branches scratching in the air like a skeleton. David shouts with excitement at the faint outline of a car fin flashing in the grey light. "Look, people are still driving!"

Like the lower bulb of an hourglass, the front window fills with snow until we can no longer see anything. David and I drag a chair from the kitchen to the living room. I hold my brother's legs as he tilts his chin and peers out.

"Can you see anything?" I ask.

"No," he whispers.

"Nothing? Not even a house?"

"It's all gone."

A voice calls from the kitchen. A question with my name attached.

"Nothing!" I answer.

Our mother comes around the corner and sees David, the chair, the putty-coloured window. She grabs the drapery wand and pulls the curtain across. According to her, heat is going right out the window.

The TV isn't working. My older brother says the aerial has been knocked down. We are allowed to play in the living room. David scatters his Lego across the carpet. He builds tall narrow towers that fall over easily. Kerry is constructing military compounds with entrances and exits. Diane is probably in her room with her new leather-cased transistor radio that she got for Christmas. I am reading *The Long Winter* in a chair in the corner. Laura Ingalls Wilder's family is trapped in a snowstorm too—Pa's playing the fiddle to keep up spirits. Our father is in a place called Virginia. He left after Christmas wearing his blue Air Force uniform with the gold buttons. We remain behind in a new city with shocking weather.

When I look up from my book—*I am not afraid of the dark, Laura said*—David is gone. His allotment of Lego is an abandoned pile of rubble. Kerry's gone too, but he's taken his half of the coloured bricks with him. In front of the window the curtain is billowing with air. I listen for the sound of the furnace, the steady hum of a motor running in the basement, but I only hear the storm outside the walls. When the fabric ripples like wind across water, I know where he is.

I slide in beside my brother. It is not so dark.

"Do you think there's anyone outside?" David whispers.

"There can't be," I say.

The wind slams the house and we laugh nervously.

David and I are the storm-watchers. We sit next to the window and listen.

Every gust of wind that shakes the house flies through our veins too. Like soothsayers we know the storm with our bodies. We press our faces to the walls and glass and feel the sting of ice reaching inside. We scrape the frost with our fingers, melting gems that drip onto the floor. When the wind shakes the window, our hands hover like sea birds. We imagine the glass curving into our palms.

"Will the house fall in?" David asks.

In the middle of the night, I fall out of bed. *Something's wrong.* I open the bedroom door and peer down the hallway. *What is it?* I walk slowly to the living room, fingertips grazing the walls in the dark. The furniture looks odd and only vaguely familiar. The red couch has swollen in the night, its cushions plump and uneven. The coffee table has sunk into the floor like it rests on quicksand. In the corner, a twisted floor lamp touches the ceiling, the yellowed shade pointing upward. *Am I still asleep?*

And then I remember. I know what is missing. I slip behind the drapes pulled shut across the front window and put my hands on the glass.

"The wind's gone," I whisper.

I wait, listening for the fine vibration of air trapped inside walls. Silence is terrifying too.

In the morning, the first sound to break through is a *whump* coming from the south side of the house. We crowd onto the small landing and watch our mother slowly open the back door. A single layer of glass belonging to the storm door is the only thing holding back a wall of packed snow. *Whump.* Someone's digging, she breathes. *Whump.* We hear the steady, hopeful sound of a metal blade attacking the substance of our entrapment.

David and I pull on our snow pants and jackets. Another sweater, our mother insists, so we take everything off and start again. We escape as soon as the scarves are wrapped twice around our heads—one band each across the bare foreheads, a second over our mouths.

When David and I push the storm door open we step into a world made of light. Snow glitters like shards of glass have fallen from the sky. Ice crystals flicker blue, pink, and green. We shield our mole-eyes and open them slowly, just half at first, squinting at the sea of white that lies before us.

"It's like a ray gun," David says, happy to burn.

No, it's another world, I think.

The neighbour who has freed us has no face, just a black balaclava and two holes for eyes. We wave at him as we crawl up the snow bank that skirts the house like a walled moat. He waves at us with giant black-mittened hands and goes back to his shovelling.

We crawl to the front yard with a three-movement rhythm: step-sink-creep, step-sink-creep, elbows and knees driving into white powder. When we get to the front street, we see what the storm has done. Houses are buried except for the roofs. On each shingled peak the wind has swept a single white wave waiting to break. The tree trunks and cars have disappeared too. Squares of coloured metal peek out of snow banks like ancient artifacts buried in sand. But the most amazing thing is that instead of a road, a frozen river stands before us—the serpentine ice flowing and twisting like a mountain stream caught between canyon walls.

We start with angels. Falling backward into soft deep drifts. *Whump.* Arms and legs together. *Flap. Flap.* The snow holds us close like arms around our waists.

We stare at a spotless sky.

"Pretend we're looking down, David. It's a blue lake, not air."

"We're flying," he says. *Flap. Flap.*

"I'm done," I say, standing up and turning to examine my angel mold. "It looks like the inside of a walnut."

"Mine's a bird," says David, struggling to rise without ruining the wings.

After pock-marking the yard with a dozen celestial bodies we crawl to where the road used to be. We run along the hard flank of the snowdrifts, screaming as we break through the overhanging cornices. I follow David. His feet kick up small tufts of snow. Blue arms swing as he skips the frozen waves. When he reaches the end of the street, he turns and calls to me.

"Ca-thy!"

"Da-vid!" I shout back.

In the still air we shout the names like we are each other's echoes.

The snow cave takes hours to dig. A narrow tunnel to get in and then a large central chamber cleared to the asphalt. We make benches to line the walls and a small raised table at the centre. For light, we punch holes in the roof with broomsticks. When it is done we admire the craftsmanship. Then we crawl out to marvel at the hidden entranceway and crawl back in for the thrill of rediscovering a room under the snow.

We trudge home when the sun starts to sink. Our cave has long collapsed. We tried to build another but the snow lost its willingness to hold a dome-shape and we grew tired from digging, our woolen mittens heavy and frozen. In the tinged pewter light of dusk, we crawl over a shelled landscape, decimated as any battlefield. The smooth lips of snowdrifts are broken. The yards all the way down the street are dotted with pits as if gophers have been set free. Tunnels have collapsed into long trenches. What had once been a scene of sculpted snow and ice is now destroyed. Everywhere I look, angels have fallen and splattered.

We had played upon it like we were sucking for air, as if beauty could be inhaled.

When we reach the back yard, we try climbing up to the roof. There is one remaining clean wave of snow untouched by our desire. Our mother tries to stop us by knocking on the storm door and waving her finger. You will sink into a snow bank, suffocate, and not be found until spring, she warns.

But for David and I, the entombment had already happened. For three days we had huddled inside a shaking house, behind frozen doors and opaque windows, next to walls of ice pressing into our bodies, until the wind found a way in. It filled us with a power we did not know before—fear and longing merging into one feeling. This is what I missed when the wind stopped.

I push my brother up the wall of snow and we jump anyway. We just have to. Feet first into a cold white sea.

WINTER SOLSTICE

Everything here is painted in the colour of water:
The books, the house, the pair of compasses,
the edge of the evening,
And around, an endless expanse,
the light of snow.

EEVA-LIISA MANNER

"MOMMY? ARE YOU AWAKE?"
"Yes. What is it, sweetie?"
"What happened to the rock?" Victoria whispers in my ear.
Her words are hot and damp.
"What rock?"
"The turtle rock. The one you put in the suitcase."
"I threw it in the ocean."
"Did you tell the ocean to give Uncle David back?"

"Yes."

"Did you yell?"

"No."

"You should have yelled, Mommy. Maybe the ocean didn't hear you."

Every night since I've returned from Madeira, my bed is filled with bodies. A tangle of arms and legs scatter across the mattress like they've been thrown here in a heap or washed up on a shore. At bedtime, I peel the children from around my neck, pull their blankets to their chins and shut their doors, but soon they are out of bed, bare feet padding across the hallway, bodies soft with flannelette reaching for me.

Tonight, the two youngest children are sleeping soundly. They look like waxen forms, moon-faces shadowed with damp strands of hair. Sam has one on each side of him. David's head hangs off the edge of the bed, saliva bubbling over his lip. Tegan's pink and white nightie bunches at her waist.

"I thought you weren't coming home, Mommy," Victoria whispers. "I dreamed you'd found Uncle David and went sailing with him."

"Go to sleep, sweetie. I'm here now." I pull her in close and rub her back.

"Don't go away again, Mommy. I don't like it."

When her breathing becomes slow and deep I lift her hand from my neck and slide her body next to her sister's. I get out of bed and look down at my family. The children are still. Sam's broad shoulder is flung back across a pillow, the pale flesh of his underarm dark with feathery hair.

I thought you weren't coming home. Sam had said something similar twelve years ago when I flew back from Athens.

I lift up my son's solid little body and turn him around, placing his head on a pillow. I tuck the duvet under four pairs of feet and leave my family to the safety of their sleep. The latch clicks as I pull the door tight against the jamb.

The upstairs hallway is filled with moonlight. Overhead, the cathedral ceiling glows blue like an Orthodox dome. I descend the stairwell, walking slowly down steps bathed in light. On the last riser, I pause. A cold draft sweeps along the floor like smoke. The front door has never been sealed properly.

In the kitchen I fill the kettle from the tap and place it over the gas ring. I turn off the overhead light and watch blue flames curl up the metal sides.

Women can go mad with insomnia.

The sleep-deprived roam houses that have lost their familiarity. With tea mugs in hand, we wander rooms, looking on shelves for something we will recognize: a book title, a photograph, the teak-carved bird—a souvenir from what place? A memory almost rises when our eyes rest on a painting's grey sweep of cloud, or the curve of a wooden table leg in a corner. Fingertips faintly recall the raised pattern on a chair cushion, but we wonder how these things have come to be here, in this stranger's home.

Lost women drift in places where time has collapsed. We look into our thoughts and hearts for what has been forgotten, for what has gone missing. What did we once care about? Whom did we love? We are emptied. We are remote. Like night lilies, we open in the dark, breathe in the shadowy world. Our soliloquies are heard by no one.

I AM FALLING. Not from a willow branch, Ophelia breaking the glassy stream open, answering the call of dead-men's-fingers, but over a sea cliff I tumble.

I see you. Body spinning like a storm cloud. Limbs flailing in the deep hollowed waves. Are you carving an angel in the water?

Your face is white, freckled as a child's. Your hair is lit with phosphorescence, the stirred creatures caught in long golden strands. You call my name, a sea name I have never heard before but know is mine. I reach for you, open palms slipping through water the colour of clouds. Your arm twists towards me, your hand is just beyond my fingertips.

Before I can get to you, a wave grows between us, dark and green, a forbidding wall rising into air. The wave crests and arcs, a perfect white curl suspended in air. Unable to hold its wind-carved shape, the wave collapses and falls like a massive boulder. The sea explodes. Silent white spray shatters the sky.

You are gone, my drowned brother.

Blackness soft as clay.

I listen in the dark. No wind or sea, no cry. Nothing.

Into what silent place have I fallen? I look to my body. I have no form, no muscle-wrapped bones, no internal organs exchanging blood and air. I am a skin waiting to be inhabited.

If I swim, I will become a sea creature. If I fly, I will grow wings. But if I remember, then what?

How do I take a shape and be alive without you?

"DIANE STILL HOPES, you know," Mom says.

"I know," I say into the phone.

"We have to wait for her."

"I know."

"To be ready."

"Yes."

It should be me, I suppose, to declare that you are not coming back. But I do not want to be the one. I want someone else to finish this story. Kerry or Diane. Mom or Dad. Another voice to say it's over, come and mourn. But no one is willing. In spite of the time that has passed and the knowledge of the storm that blasted through the North Atlantic in September, our family is not ready. We are trapped in the terrible silence of muted grief and disbelief.

We are waiting for one of us to speak first. Or for some-one to break down—uncontrollable sobs, wailing. Is it the *feeling* of hope we are reluctant to abandon, that light that keeps the darkness from creeping in, our family island still lit with the idea of you?

Hope is a fierce longing. It can beat your heart for months.

Kerry is determined to find something.

He's contacted a salvage operator out of New York, a man who makes his living off the sea by scavenging the remains of wrecked or discarded marine vessels. The man seems to think it's possible that *Mugwump* is still out there—an empty yacht drifting towards Bermuda. What does that mean? You and Sarah were swept overboard? You abandoned *Mugwump* too early? Didn't you know you were supposed to step *up* to the life raft?

For a while Dad was chasing down his MP and the Department of External Affairs. "Why don't they goddamn do something?" was the chorus at the beginning of November. But now he is quiet, his feelings going underground. Even he cannot sustain the rant. "We'll just have to wait," is all he says when I telephone. He quickly passes the phone to Mom.

Mom and I speak most days, though there are no encour-aging details left. Hope once had its own tongue. We repeated the precious phrases like mantras. *There are provisions for eight weeks on board. She was built to do this kind of sailing.* We hung our future selves on them, like a much-loved sweater we would never throw out.

We miss our convictions and long for a previous life when we believed in possibility.

Sometimes she cries.

"Why did he do this to me?" she whispers. "If he knew how much he was hurting me, he never would have gone sailing."

I want to argue that you didn't care what any of us thought. Yet I don't. In spite of her pain, Mom seems to gain comfort in believing that her suffering would have mattered to you.

"He didn't mean for this to happen, Mom," I say. *We can't make this about us,* I want to add. But how else do we make sense of it at all?

"What did he mean then by not telling us?"

"He didn't want you to worry. He didn't want to hear your fears."

"But I would have been right to worry."

We thought we were special, David. Always believing we were the brave ones in the family. The ones so assured we didn't look for advice. And because we often had each other's approval we didn't need our parents or siblings to understand our motivations.

We were so adept at avoiding conflict we didn't even see the cost to ourselves. Our growing isolation.

TIME PASSES SLOWLY IN November. December. Pale sunlight. Lengthening nights. In the mornings I rise in the dark and shake the children awake. I choose their clothes if they can't decide what to wear and then we find our way downstairs in socks. In the kitchen, I tuck cereal boxes under an arm and lift the plastic milk jug with one finger. Spoons and bowls clatter on the table. The children eat with purpose. Slurping. Crunching. I blank out the sounds and listen to the hum of the furnace. It's comforting, the way the warm air swirls at our feet. If we stay inside we won't freeze.

Usually, I linger at the kitchen table and we are too late to walk to school. I drive the five blocks, take the children to their classes and hug them tightly. Victoria squirms. David hugs back harder. Tegan smiles. I hold my children close to me and listen for their breathing. But then the great emptiness starts to grow, the blackness, the void, and I cannot hold them any longer. I let my children fall away.

In the front foyer of the school I wave off invitations for coffee at Bell's. I can no longer sustain a conversation. I hear only the echo, not the speaker's voice. Sometimes I catch the conjunctions—*the*, *and*, *or*—the connecting words, but to what? The sentences are unrecognizable, like a foreign language I've never bothered to learn. Someone asks a question, a reply is expected, but I don't know what we're talking about.

I park the car at the end of 14th Street, dodge the unleashed dogs running like greyhounds and head for the ravine. I walk as close to the edge as I dare. My feet slide. Clumps of crumbled earth slide down to the river.

I have returned to a land with three horizons. The first is a line of stubbled earth—the prairie fields broken and turned, lying fallow until spring. The second is the ragged bite of mountains, the stately wall of rock running north and south. But the third line is made of air: A chinook arch—purple and grey clouds smudged across the upper half of a clear sky, the underside marked with a dark band as blue as a vein under the tongue. It reminds me of another demarcation not visible here—the sea-darkened curve where sailors fall off and women stare over the edge.

I still look for you. Keep my eye out for a boat with red and white sails, hovering along a horizon.

A magpie flies over my head, mocking my despair with a piercing tongue. I pick up a stone and fling it at the plump black body. I miss but the bird leaves, crying. The colour blue flashes under its wing.

THE YEAR HAS BEEN too hard.

It begins in winter with a white shirt. Collar buttons unable to slide into their narrow stitched slits. The diagnosis of Sam's cancer. Surgery. The angry red scar. And then the radiation treatment that sends Sam and I to separate beds. In the spring, we are blindsided again. This time it's by something small and red, a cherry jujube.

"Hey lady, there's something wrong with her." A boy with wet hair tugs at my sleeve. I turn away from the swimmers behind the glass and see Tegan flapping her arms and running in a tight circle. Her mouth is open but she's not making a sound.

I pick her up and run down the hallway, throwing her across the front counter into the arms of a lifeguard.

"She's choking!" I shout.

The woman looks in her mouth, squeezes her sternum, turns her upside down but the breathless colour continues to spread. Her arms are putty grey. Her face looks like it's been dyed with a thin wash of indigo. And still there's no sound.

"Where is she?" Sam's voice breaks through the silence. Victoria's cry hovers at my left hip. And now I hear everything.

The sound of running shoes on linoleum.

A hair dryer blowing hot air.

A little boy whining for a drink.

Strangers whisper, *What's happening? What's wrong with her?*

The lifeguards talk in short, intense phrases.

"Hit her again."

"Do we need 911?"

"Make the call."

Tegan's eyes lock with mine, plead with me. Air. Voice. Cry.

There is nothing. There is no way to make a sound when the throat is jammed.

I will time to slow down. How long has it been? One minute? Two minutes? Not three already? A lifeguard flips her over—a hand hits her back—a door swings open—a hand hits her back—a siren wails along the tree-lined street—a hand hits her back—the siren is in the parking lot—a hand hits her back—the eyes close, the lashes wet—and then the candy shoots out like a clump of red wax.

Her cry fills my body.

Violence wakes in me. I grab my daughter and drag her over the counter, not caring that her feet catch on the counter ledge and a shoe is wrenched free. I hold her shuddering body next to my own. My limbs fill with heat like lava has burst out of a cleft in my heart. Fear burns under my skin, not relief. White hot fear. I recognize the sensation. And the unspoken truth. Death is our constant shadow.

Later, the next day, the next month, Sam and I don't speak of Tegan's blue skin. Neither one of us dares to ask out loud: What if she died? What if she was brain-damaged? Like the other question we don't ask—what if the cancer comes back?

We think that if we don't name our fears, they can have no power.

Silence maroons us to separate islands.

SAM IS HAPPY TONIGHT when he enters the house humming Christmas songs, singing the odd line. *Good King Wenceslas....* I stand in the hallway and stare at him like he's a stranger coming in the front door. A dark bristle shadows the lower half of his face. *When did he stop shaving?*

"They'll probably end up having to glue a beard on me," he says to the children. "Jesus's father must look manly." He strokes his cheeks, patchy with soft brown whiskers. Oh, I remember now, the Christmas play at the children's school. That time of year already.

"Ollie. What's the matter?" He lengthens his chin, scratches his head, and looks puzzled. Stan Laurel is back. I've not seen him stretch his face into this character for a long while.

"Are they making you sing, Daddy?" Victoria asks while David swings on Sam's flexed arm, his knees dragging across the wood floor.

"Nope. I just don't sing, I told them. Except in the shower, of course, where I am rather good. But the director is letting me speak the lines."

"Does everyone else have to sing?" asks Victoria.

"Everyone but me."

I imagine Sam at centre-stage, a bearded, faithful Joseph holding his blonde Mary, her blue-cloaked body leaning into his arms while she sings of the child she is to bear.

"You're too scared to sing," David says.

Sam strokes Mary's head.

"Let's just say I'm doing the audience a favour. So who's ticklish tonight?"

"Me!"

"Me!"

"I think...Mommy's ticklish!" His hands reach for the caves of my armpits but I cross my arms, pressing my elbows into my breasts.

"I don't like being tickled. Please stop," I plead. But he is strong and manages to slide some fingers under the thick tendon in the curve of my arm. He pinches hard. "Sam, please stop it."

"You're no fun, Mommy," David says, fluttering his fingers across my stomach.

"Yeah. Lighten up," Sam laughs while he comes at me from behind, squeezing the soft flesh at my waist. My stomach flinches, the muscles retract towards the spine.

My God, will he try to tickle Mary too?

"I'm tired, okay?" I push his hand away as hard as I can and climb the stairs, feet kicking against the white stair plate. I feel my face grow hot with anger and shame. *It's just a game. It's just for fun.* But my body hurts.

Don't anyone touch me! The voice hammers in my skull.

I slam the door and stand in the middle of the room. *Mugwump* could have fit in here. Why did we build such a large bedroom?

I am missing how I used to believe in this life.

ON THE SHORTEST DAY of the year the sun rises so late I wonder if it will show at all. It is half past eight before it bursts the dusty eastern line. The sky is faded, pale as if the blue has been leached away. It will not be much of a day.

I carry my brother's letters to the table and let them slide across the glass. I open the envelopes slowly, reading the back flaps where on every one he printed his name and a country. New Zealand. Australia. Japan. Thailand. Nepal. India. I imagine this as his favourite part in the art of letter writing. He licks the yellow glue with his tongue, rubs a finger along the V, and seals the envelope shut. And then he writes where he is in the world. China.

There is a place that I can visualize in my mind, pictures drawn from the recollection of childhood, but nonetheless real to me. I see the changing of the seasons of that mindful place—the wondrous activity of spring, summer, and fall—but under a blanket of snow, the earth sleeping as a child, winter is the most beautiful of all. I daydream about a crisp winter's day, the snow crunching beneath my boots, a shiver running down my spine. For the first time in weeks I feel cool. I glance at the cane-covered hills and the heat returns. How lovely they would look with a light dusting of snow.

I fold the letter but keep it in my hand while I look through the archway leading into the living room. Tegan is at the front window. She stands silent—hands and face pressed up against the glass—and then slips behind the curtains. Her small body is just a shadow under the long striped sheers. Her leg moves, silk ripples like a veil. I wonder if she's looking at the tree, the twisted ash, the dark clumps of berries—or is she watching for the first snowflakes?

How lovely it would look with a light dusting....

I need it to snow, David. I need a storm to hide the world as we once knew it. Snow to cover the earth, blanket the debris of a dead autumn. I need winter to blow in and mark the change of seasons—that was when we loved and hoped, this is when all is lost.

At the window, there are now two bodies playing under the curtains. David has joined his sister. But unlike Tegan he is not trying to hide. Instead, David runs from the window with his hands stretched out, pushing the sheer panel up until it appears to float over his head. His knees slide across the floor. When he stops moving, he gets up and does it again. And again. He'd do it all day if I let him. Or until disaster strikes and the curtain is torn from the rod.

"WHY DO KIDS LOVE TO do the same things over and over?" you ask, while playing a clapping game with your one-year-old niece. You are tiring of it and trying to interest her in something else but she can't be swayed.

"More,"Victoria says, reaching for your hands and pressing them together.

"Okay, once more, and then we'll play Uncle David has a beer," you tell her, slapping her little hands in a confused game of patty-cake with the baker's man bringing you a Labatt's.

"Why do they like repetition?" you muse.You flip the beer cap into the air and catch it. "Are neural pathways developing future patterned behaviours, or is it just the pleasure of rhythm?"

"More," Victoria yells. And you spin the cap again, this time across the kitchen.

What I want to know is, when.

What day, what time, what moment?

Where was I? What was I doing? Sleeping? Dreaming?

Did any part of my body register you falling?

I am missing you, David. I want to ask you something. What were you thinking when your body slipped into the cold sea?

Tegan is standing still like a silk-wrapped pillar. She has spun herself around until she's cocooned. David is running from under the other curtain towards me. His arms are up, the sheers fluttering behind him like a cape.

Patterns or rhythms? you asked me. Or is it skin? Does your niece love the feel of silk against her face? Does your nephew want the rush of air? I reach for him, but he slips away.

IN THE AFTERNOON I call Diane, catch her while she's pushing Mark around the house.

"Go fast," I hear my nephew say. Diane gives his wheelchair a spin. I imagine the spokes blurring into liquid.

"What kind of day is Winnipeg having?" I ask.

"Overcast," she says. "Calgary?"

"The light is flat."

"Go fast," Mark says again. "Go fast." I see him lowering his chin to cover the hole in his trachea.

"Just a second, Cath. Mark needs another turn." Diane puts the phone down. I hear her running shoes squeak across the kitchen linoleum like small frightened animals.

Mark can make a few phrases to announce his pleasures and desires. *Living Room. Hockey. Go away.* But *Go fast* is his favourite. If he had his way, his day would be spent wheeling through the maze of rooms and hallways—starting in the kitchen, down the hall, around the living room, into the elevator, and finally arriving in the open space of the cool basement. He'd travel this route all day if he could, never stopping. Perhaps it's the movement of air across his face that he likes, a breeze, a waft, a gust of wind against his skin. *Go fast.* Or does he understand, in the deep cells of his eight-year-old quadriplegic body, that life is movement, and it is our greatest desire?

"I've been skimming through *Adrift*, again," Diane says. "Do you realize the man caught birds with his hands?"

I've read the survival book too. Jo had a copy on *Columban*. It's a true story about a sailboat breaking apart west of Madeira, possibly by a whale or a floating container. The North Equatorial current carried the life raft eighteen hundred miles to the Guadeloupe Islands where fishermen found the sailor seventy-six days later.

For a time, the book had given me hope as well.

"The human spirit is extraordinary," Diane says.

"The guy's will was certainly strong," I say. "But maybe he had some luck. A sea current carried him into the path of the fishing boat."

"I don't believe in luck."

"How about Fate?"

"No. But I think the universe will come to our aid if we trust in its power."

A power willing to create and destroy.

I want to tell Diane that it's over for me. Even if you and Sarah had managed to climb into a life raft, it's been 112 days since *Mugwump* left Ireland.

I want to let you go, but to abandon hope is to abandon our sister as well. Diane has believed in the impossible long before you went sailing. Mark's a miracle, she once told me. He was never supposed to live.

Until you went missing, I didn't understand how our sister managed the world of her disabled child with its daily reminder of the fragility of the body. But now I've come to realize that the shadow of death is not the force hovering in her home—it is Life that powers through Mark's veins—the precious breath his mother watches over, every minute of the day.

In Diane's world, every intake of air, every shake of Mark's head, every word her son brings forth from the hole in his throat

is full of meaning. And with meaning there is purpose and a reason to Life. In your world, David, you expected life to be a
vigorous force to wrestle with, and out of the doing and survival
of the task, meaning would come. But it turns out, you and
Diane believe the same thing—true freedom is in the awareness
of the whole and present moment, whether it is the recognition
of a child's soul or the ability to stay alive with hands and wits.

"Di...," I begin, my head heavy, as if fog is swirling in
thick wafts. I am unable to make the pronouncement but she
knows what I want to say anyway.

"I hope it was merciful," Diane whispers, "at the end." I
hear the weariness in her voice, the slow movement of the
tongue making the syllables too soft against the teeth. And
then I hear her swallow.

I hope it was the beginning of September, David. Under
the gales. A soft fall.

AT DUSK, THERE IS winter in the air.

A friend enters my house. Snow crosses the threshold with
her, blowing like coarse salt. The ice crystals bounce across the
floor.

"This isn't like Winnipeg snow," I say, and my body starts
to shake. She shuts the door and leads me to a chair by the
window.

Outside the sky darkens. Dusty lilac, grey.

"It wasn't much of sunset," I whisper. No horizon slicing
through the fat curves of an orange ball, no golden fingertip
pared away. The star simply collapsed. Ash instead of a yellow
glow spread across the low hung sky. On the shortest day of the
year, that was all the light we got.

I begin to cry and cannot stop. My body shudders, small
depth charges exploding under my skin. I feel my friend's

hands on my head. She is stroking my hair, over and over like I've done for my children.

She opens her purse and takes out a hairbrush. The bristles scrape my skin. Catch in the tangles at the neck. Rip the hair.

The violence is shocking at first. Painful but I wish it hurt even more.

Is there blood?—there should be blood.

My friend brushes my hair from the crown to the nape, her free hand shadowing the strokes, smoothing the strands in her palm. The more I cry, the faster she pulls on the small black handle. Her rhythms match my convulsing chest, sorrow's cadence beating time. Yet I will not be calmed.

I wonder if my sister is crying.

A prairie away.

Her dark hair pulled in grief.

With the final brushstroke the hair offers no resistance. The tangles are loosened. The knots undone. The bristles slide over the ends and my hair flies up as if a wind has entered the darkening room.

Hope is a vapour, David. It dissipates the moment it leaves the body.

II

ICE

I am haunted by waters.

Norman Maclean

"So much snow," I whisper.

I roll down the window. The tires crunch over a layer of ice embedded with gravel but the silence is there, hanging over the valley like someone has whispered, *Hush*.

"It's the elevation," says Sam, after taking a sharp left turn. He presses on the accelerator and the truck rides up a steep incline.

I consider the shoulderless road. One lane runs alongside a treeless slope, ruffles of avalanche tracks scarring the snow. The opposite lane edges only air—the mountainside plunging to a valley of lakes, unblemished discs of frozen white. There is no place to pull over on this highway.

"I think the sky is darker here. Like in Nepal," Sam says. "Remember Machapuchre?"

I remember. A fishtail peak, bright as a storm-lit sail. Spindrifts of snow had swept the cerulean sky. We loved those mountains.

When the highway dips and turns, Tegan giggles and says, "There are holes in my stomach!"

"You know, pretty soon we're going to have more time to spend together as a family," says Sam, his eyes glancing at the rearview mirror and then across to me. I know he wants to believe this statement but it doesn't seem very likely. Sam likes to work. His discontent in Calgary isn't about the hours his accounting firm demands.

"I WANT TO BUY a hotel," he says to me in early January. "I'm tired of the corporate world. I want my own thing, my own work that will create something that lasts. For me. For us." He smiles.

This is not a new idea. He's looked for years for the right venture but in the last six months he's been silent on the matter. His cancer scare and the missing *Mugwump* kept us busy—not much time was spent thinking about the future.

I look at him across the kitchen table and have two thoughts: We all deserve our dreams, and, how do I say no to this one? There have been other entrepreneurial opportunities Sam was interested in but they meant moving either to Dallas or Miami. I resisted uprooting our family but buying a hotel in the mountains, a few hours away, seems to be a plausible idea. We won't have to move. The kids will attend the same school. In the beginning, Sam will be absent from the city but we'll have the weekends together. It won't be much different than now. And there is something else. I wonder what it would be like to live in the cold beauty of the Rocky Mountains. To have such quiet in the air. Can we escape to this place together and heal our wounds?

The road winds under the towering peaks of the Icefields Parkway.

In the summer, this valley will be green—forests of pine, mossy lakes glowing like gems—but in March, the terrain is one colour and one texture. Bleached mountain meadows, snow-laden fir trees, rocky summits layered and softened by wind-forming cornices of ice. A white blanket covering the land.

When we reach the two-toed Crowfoot Glacier, Victoria shouts, "There it is!" The red roof floats on the snow, the only colour we've seen in the last forty kilometres.

The scene is beautiful. Bow Lake is an almost perfect circle of white ice. Grey mountains to the south and west slope away from the shore. Bow Glacier hangs between two peaks. The buildings are set back from the lake, nestled in a forest of pine trees, boughs heavy with snow. The hotel is isolated and appears like a gift—a tired traveller would rejoice to come upon such a place in the middle of nowhere.

At the access road, we turn off the highway and drive through a corridor of ten-foot snowbanks. Sam nudges the truck into a corner of the parking lot. We stare at the hotel through the windshield. It is stately but rustic. Up close the red shingles are faded. The logs are dark and stained. A wooden sign with the words, Num-ti-Jah, is nailed above the entrance. This is Sam's dream. A twenty-six-room lodge, 6,500 feet above sea level.

We walk around the building before going in. The children find crystals in the rocks glued to the window ledges. David presses his face to a window. "There's a bunch of animal heads in there," he shouts. We make the circle, admiring the peaked rooflines, the log construction, and arrive back at the entranceway where thick plastic is stretched over a plywood vestibule. It bulges like a bullfrog's throat when we push the wide door open.

Mountains are quiet in the winter. And the hotel is no different—a hush of dust and aged soot hangs in the air. We wander the vacant halls and rooms. Chairs are turned over onto tabletops. Sagging box springs on metal frames dip to the floor. Stained mattresses curl away from the walls. On the third floor, David hides behind a door and jumps out. Victoria screams, "It's haunted!" Her piercing voice is swallowed into the orange carpeting and cheap panelled walls of the attic floor. Tegan hangs onto my jacket, wide-eyed and saying nothing.

"Do you remember it being so dark?" Sam asks when we make our way down the creaking stairs.

I nod. But strangely remember little else. Yet this is where Sam and I spent our honeymoon weekend nine years ago.

ON FRIDAY AFTERNOONS, I pack up our winter clothes and drive two-and-a-half hours into the mountains. I try to get to the lodge before the sunlight fades. In total darkness, I can feel the mountains press over Bow Valley like giants touching their heads together. My eyes follow the car's beams but there's little to see in the falling light except the twists and turns of the black roadway and the white banks of snow fading to grey. I drive with both hands on the steering wheel and glance down at the slow spin of the odometer. When we arrive, the children open the car doors before I've even stopped at the back entrance. I call them back for their bags and they drag the coloured duffles across the icy parking lot. Inside the lodge, they look for Sam by screaming, "Daddy!" Some nights he greets them with exuberant bear hugs. Other times he tells them to be quiet. "There are guests," he says tersely.

Sam is absorbed with transforming himself into an innkeeper. There has been more work and more problems than he could have imagined: the generator needs constant maintenance; the heating system is impossible to fine tune—there is hot and off; the kitchen is over forty years old and the chef is complaining daily; the staff love the remoteness of Bow Lake but need to drink to check their evening boredom; the original owners, who live on-site and act as if the hotel still belongs to them, are sometimes difficult with their criticism. Sam juggles it all including the worry that this run-down old lodge can actually turn a profit. The children and I rarely see him. If he's not in the office he is scurrying along a hallway to the latest crisis or taking someone on a tour. Sometimes he's able to join us for a meal in the dining room but we are often interrupted with a guest's demands, a mechanical breakdown, or a staff problem.

This is the reality of his dream.

On Sunday nights the children and I return to the city.

The rhythm of our life is now a family separated by mountains. As I climb into the car, bracing for the long ride home through the darkening valley, I repeat the statement I am trying to believe in: We all deserve the chance to follow our ambitions, no matter what the outcome. But as each week passes my conviction wanes. Adventurers and entrepreneurs don't always consider the effects of their choices. And for those left behind there is the shameful question: Were we abandoned for the dream?

When we get home, David slides in beside Tegan in her bed. His sister is already holding her favourite book about a rottweiler named Carl. The picture book without words tells the story of a mother who leaves her baby in the care of the family pet.

"When Daddy doesn't live with us anymore, can we get a Carl dog?" David asks.

"We can't get a dog, David!" Victoria shouts from the hallway. She is sitting on the floor with the door slightly ajar. She won't come into Tegan's room because she's angry. I had forgotten about a birthday party and by the time she reminded me it was too late to go shopping. She had refused to go without a present. Still, she loves the *Carl* books, so she's listening through the crack.

I go on with the story, giving a deep voice to the dog. David's favourite part is when the rottweiler pushes the child down the laundry chute. Tegan likes it when the baby is allowed to swim in the fish tank. I smile at the dancing dog, up on his hind legs. Victoria pretends to accidentally push the door open with her foot. I turn the book towards her.

"Leave the hall light on, Mommy," Victoria says later when I tuck her into bed. She hugs me for a long time.

When the children are asleep I go down to the kitchen. Instead of doing the dishes, I open a map of the North Atlantic on the table. I trace my finger along the western shore of Ireland. From Castletownbere, *Mugwump* motors through the narrow strait that separates Bere Island from the Beara Peninsula. Once past Ardnakinna Point the sails are raised and the boat heads for Sheeps Head. A day later, Mizen Head is to stern. And then, nothing. The ocean shrugs and swallows the small yacht.

This is the nightly ritual.

I open the weather report I requested from the London Meteorological Office. I consider the wave heights between September 1 and September 10. I read David's letters over and over again, searching for some foreshadowing of what was to happen.

Our confidence in ourselves had grown in just two weeks, but our confidence in Mugwump *has increased tenfold. Never once did she seem to be stressed or out of control despite some of our bad seamanship. She just seemed to quietly go about her business. Though she's small, we felt very comfortable; she doesn't leak (much), all her systems work fine and she's easy to handle. As a bonus she looks great, wherever we go people comment on her looks and her name.*

"Mommy?"

The learning curve is steep on these first cruises and we certainly learned a lot. Funny thing was we always assumed everyone had more experience than us yet we saw some terrible examples of bad seamanship. We're feeling very encouraged about going further afield next year.

"Mommy, I'm thirsty."

How's the Uncle David Clan doing? Sorry I can't be there to see them growing up, but maybe next year we'll all be sailing on Mugwump.

I run the water from the tap until it is cool. I fill a pink plastic cup and pass it to Tegan. She takes one sip, gives it back to me and runs back to bed.

David went sailing, I stayed home to raise three children.

My brother believed an existence of quiet desperation was to be avoided at all costs. To keep moving was the definition of being alive. One's achievements should be measured by physical and mental strength.

David pitted himself against Nature—raw, wild and unpredictable, while I was doing laundry and reading children stories.

In different circumstances my brother may have survived his voyage. I could still be crushed in the Subaru on a mountain highway. So, who has lived with more risk? Or who has lost more?

I have been too afraid to look at these questions. Magnifying glasses can start fires. Landscapes scorched. Families left homeless. Isn't it necessary sometimes to look away before regret takes hold?

I have often envied him. The dream. The desire. The bravery. I wanted freedom too. But women bound to children and men are forced to fly in smaller circles.

ON A SATURDAY AT the lodge, I find Sam working at two in the morning. From the reception area I can see into the small office crammed with two desks. Blocks of coloured file folders are piled on the polished surfaces like giant puzzle pieces. In the middle of the room, Sam is standing on the only piece of carpet that isn't covered with documents. Holding a stack of paper in his arms, he peels off the top sheet and puts the item onto a categorized pile. Bills—paid, unpaid. Payroll. Reservations. Receipts. Taxes. Two filing cabinet drawers sit open revealing more file folders waiting to offer the documents a permanent home.

"Why aren't you sleeping?" he asks, looking up.

"Can't."

"God, it's all I want to do."

"It's the altitude, I think." Six thousand and five hundred feet of awakeness. "Why don't you go to bed?"

"There's too much to do," he says, turning back to his work.

He reaches forward and slides a pale yellow receipt into a manila file, then leans back and drops a sheet onto a thick stack of airmail thin paper. I imagine the piles of paper growing with the speed of bamboo.

"Did you used to work in a post office?" I ask. His hands sort with quick flips of the wrist.

"If I could just clean this up I'd have a new lease on life." He makes a fist and pumps the air.

"Does the paper actually leave this office or does it just get moved around?"

"You know accountants. We keep records." He spins around and places some pink sheets at his feet.

I leave him swinging a fistful of envelopes back and forth. He looks like a boxer in a ring, dancing around an invisible opponent.

"Leave a path so you can get out, Sam."

The fireplace in the library is cold. I stir the ashes, looking for an ember I can get going. There are brief flashes of red but they fade when the poker touches them.

The hotel is quiet. I'm the only one awake now. Sam has gone to bed, barely making a dent in the paper management. I'm not much help to him in the office but I am organizing the redecorating and writing the new advertising copy. I think my real role here is as night watchman—the ideal job for an insomniac.

I walk through the hallways. Gloom everywhere, not just in the corners and stairwells where shadows unfold like handkerchiefs, but in the open places too. Murky ribbons funnel through the library, spectres passing through. I run my hands along the log walls, fingers tracing the chinking. The timber is warm but I feel the shifts in temperature. Icy air swirls at the windows. Warm currents and cold currents, like swimming in a lake.

On the second floor, I make a wrong turn and for a moment I am disoriented. The doors have switched numbers or moved places along the wall, or a corridor has opened up where previously there was none. Something isn't right. Either my mind has forgotten the floor plan or I've altered space.

I recall *Columban*. The thin seal that split and let the water in. I had believed last November that my energy had caused the leak. I still wonder if structures are altered by their inhabitants or is it the other way around? Do buildings and boats affect the metabolisms of those who breathe inside their walls? I lift my hair away from my neck and hear the snap of static. When I swallow, my throat catches. This morning I noticed the skin under my eyes becoming thin, like I am shrinking.

In the kitchen, I open the door of the walk-in fridge and put an industrial-sized box of plastic wrap on the floor to keep it from closing. There's a door handle on the inside but I don't trust it. Stephen King was inspired by an old hotel, and with good reason. I scoop out a generous helping of the chef's chocolate mousse—lately the only concession to coming to this place. I carry the bowl to the dining hall.

The eyes of the moose follow me as I circle the room. The kids don't like sitting at the table under his head—they complain snot will drip from his long nose onto their plates. The Rocky Mountain sheep trophy is my favourite—the ridged horns spiral backwards along the sides of the head like the adornment of a Greek god's helmet. The strangest sight is the diorama of white ptarmigans camouflaged in a winter scene. Two birds stand in fake snow, frozen for posterity.

I scrape the last bit of chocolate from the bottom of the bowl. The spoon rattles against the china, echoes in the large room. Taxidermy is an extraordinary craft—the dead embalmed for display and wonder. I stare at an elk's head, imagining the slight flare of a nostril, a closing eyelid, and then the rest of the body bursting through the wall.

"Isn't Daddy eating with us, Mommy?" David asks at six-thirty on a Saturday night.

"He'll be along when he can."

"Like never," mutters Victoria.

"Can we get a dog, Mommy?"

"No."

"Can I have dessert instead of dinner?" asks Tegan.

"No."

"Mom, there's another birthday party next weekend and I have to go."

"I know, Victoria. We won't be coming up next weekend."

"But, Daddy will miss us," says Tegan.

"Amanda says there's a ghost in room sixteen," David says, his hands shaking next to his face, eyes wide. "Things are moving around in the room."

Sam arrives when the food is cold. He sits down but turns his chair so he can face both the entrance to the restaurant and the double doors that lead to the kitchen.

"So, what's new, kids?" he asks.

"Nothing," says Victoria, slouching in a chair.

"We're getting a dog," David announces.

"No, we're not," Victoria replies in a sing-song voice. "Daddy's allergic."

"But he could live outside," David pleads.

"He can't live outside all the time," Sam explains. "It's just too cold."

"He could have a dog house, Daddy."

"Like a log cabin, Sam," I add. "With a red shingled roof."

Sam glares at me. "Why are you encouraging this? We can't have a dog. You know this."

I do know this. I don't even want a dog. It's just something else to take care of, but the dog thing is a jab to let him know I'm not happy. What I really want to say is the hotel was a bad idea, let's cut our losses and go home. We shouldn't be living like this.

"I'll be right back," Sam says. He walks across the dizzying patterned carpet towards the kitchen. He pushes hard against the swinging doors and almost knocks over a waiter balancing a large round tray filled with dinners.

"I'm done, Mommy," says Tegan. The sauce-free spaghetti is grey under the low-wattage bulbs. The food has been stirred but not eaten.

David slides off the vinyl chair seat and starts running out of the restaurant. "Let's play pool," he says to his sisters.

"Only if there are no guests in the lounge," I call after them.

I sit at the table and rearrange the cutlery. I line up the knives, the serrated edges facing the same way, and stack spoons one on top of another. What is there to do about this? Sam deserves to create his own work, but I'm tired, bone-tired, and every night I look around, find myself alone and wonder what happened to my idea of a family.

When Sam returns to the table we say little to each other. He fiddles with the silverware too. I stare at the white table-cloth. In the corner of my eye, a candle flame jumps and twists.

When the waiter drops an armload of plates behind me I knock over my wine glass, sending it into a roll. Sam grabs it before it hits the floor. I am reminded that in a pitching vessel, nothing is secure.

AFTER THE SURGERY, I watch Sam's face for signs that he's waking.

His eyes open and close like a puppeteer is hiding behind the hospital bed pulling the strings. The anaesthetic is starting to wear off but he's still trapped in the thick mire of propofol.

For over an hour Sam flings his head back and forth like he's trying to shake off a feeling of helplessness. He moans—a sound I've never heard him make before. I can't tell if it's pain or confusion. I examine the colour of the bandage: is there a faint yellow stain spreading at the throat?

When he starts to makes gurgling sounds I insist someone look at him.

"It sounds like he's choking," I say over the counter at the nurse's station.

She follows me into the room, takes his vitals.

"He's fine," she says, staring at her watch.

I can't stand her calmness. My heart is thumping.

When Sam is fully awake he can't speak. So, I talk to him, tell stories, chatter about the children. He watches my face. Doesn't take his eyes off me. We look at each other with the focus of new lovers.

At midnight, I ask a nurse to bring in a bed for me. I can't bear to leave him alone. Someone must listen for his breath.

For a few months after, the cancer enthralls us. We use life-affirming words like *gratitude, humbleness, family,* but they don't stick. By summer, Sam's attention has shifted to a far-off horizon. There's something he's seen beyond the frame of his life, and the children and I move to the periphery of his landscape. In the fall, I have a larger crisis to fill my mind and I turn from the growing silence at home to an ocean. Now it is winter and there is a mountain lodge—a fresh distraction, a new environment in which to spill our energies. And I am the one staring off into space.

THE PILOT FOLLOWS THE Assiniboine River east, flying low over a grid of Air Force housing before veering north to the Winnipeg terminal. My father is waiting at the bottom of the escalator, his trademark driving cap pulled low over the eyes. A long strand of white hair escapes from under the band. As the last corrugated step of the escalator collapses, he lifts the cap, runs a palm over his head, and fixes the comb-over.

"Well, Cath. You're here," he laughs. "Isn't that something?" His broad smile is filled with great looking teeth. I look for signs of aging since I last saw him in October. Is he smaller?

We stand in front of the luggage conveyor belt snaking its way through the arrivals hall.

"What colour's your suitcase?"

"Brown. Grey. Maybe taupe is the right word."

"Some people tie ribbons so they can find them easier."

"There, that one, Dad. But let me."

"No, no. I've got it," he says. He grabs the handle but the bag keeps moving. "Get out of my way," he says angrily to the row of people standing in front of the belt. He runs along with the bag and then with a jerk heaves it onto the floor.

"What's in there? Rocks?"

"Sorry. I really need to learn to pack lighter."

When we get to the house, my mother is waiting at the

kitchen window. Her hand raps on the glass followed by a quick wave. Then she's at the door holding the aluminum storm open while I drag the suitcase up the back step.

"It's good you're here," she says, hugging me tightly, crying. "It's good you've come home."

I sit down on the kitchen stool and bang my head on the rotary-dial wall phone behind me. I always forget it's there.

"Tea?" my mother asks.

Each of the mugs I bring down from the cupboard has a small crack or chip. I put them back and look for three different ones. While I'm examining an earthenware cup showcasing two Canada geese in full flight, she says, "Not those, Cathy. Get the Royal Albert out of the china cabinet. It's a special day. You're here."

I get down on my knees and squeeze between the dining room table and the cabinet. The fluted cups with the delicate handles are on the bottom shelf. They're designed for women who sip rather than drink.

"Whoa, the good ones," my father laughs as I pass him one. "Are we expecting the Queen?"

I hit my back on a chair seat when I stand up.

We'd all rather have the mugs.

I stay perched on the stool with the two small steps while my parents sit at the dinette set that followed us with three Air Force transfers. The table with the fold-out leaves features in many of our old family photos—my father with a large carving knife in his hand, my mother in an apron, the children's chins just barely above the table edge. The original Arborite top was replaced years ago when my father wanted to modernize but not get rid of a perfectly good table. Our teacups now sit on a faux wood grain.

"How did six of us ever sit around the table?" I ask, trying to imagine our nightly dinners in this little kitchen.

"Cath, come see what I've done downstairs," says my father.

He switches on the light in the rec room. A fluorescent tube hums, flickers, and goes bright. The L-shaped room with fake wood panelling and squares of white ceiling tiles hasn't changed much except for a long table, chest high, with ovals of black track winding across it. My father flips a switch and one of the engines starts to move. A little headlight in the front glows white.

The train goes slowly, pulling a long line of cars. It passes some of my brothers' Dinky toys parked in a farm scene. The scale is off but they add colour. A ten-foot-long panoramic photo of a mountain is attached to the wall at the table height. In a downtown scene there are some plastic people frozen mid-movement. A man crossing a street with a briefcase. A woman with a purse and child in opposite hands. I watch the train circle the table. Not going anywhere really. The imaginary passengers are having a boring trip. There's nothing much to see out the windows. Cardboard buildings, fake trees, giant faces staring down. The train goes around and around and around.

David believed most people's lives are just like this.

At five, the clock in the dining room chimes a brief melody of eight notes, neither mournful nor cheerful, a tentative expression of the achievement of the hour. *It is the hour, the hour is here,* it seems to ring. On the fifth strike, my older brother opens the back door. I slide off my seat, put the Royal Albert cup on the table and go to him.

"Hey, sis."

"I'm so glad I still have a brother," I blurt out.

My heart beats as I hug him. *You remain. The practical one.*

"Yeah," he says. "Yeah."

There's another day, just like this one. A winter afternoon. Steam from the kettle frosts the kitchen windows. Kerry stamps the snow off his boots in the back hall. It's the first time I've seen my brother since his infant son, Lee, died. He is thirty-three and has already lost a child.

After dinner my mother asks Kerry to bring in the laundry from outside. "You know I hate doing that," he says.

"It's okay. I'll get them," I say, grabbing one of Dad's jackets from the back hall closet. I slip my feet into his too-large shoes, open the door, and clump across the concrete to the four-sided clothesline. The tea towels are hard. The sheets are cold and fleshy. My mother's polyester pants, though, are soft and oddly warm. I unclip the clothes-pegs, leaving the wooden fingers on the rubber lines, and put the laundry in the basket. It's piled twice as high as it should be. The fabrics seem to have absorbed the ice crystals of the winter's night. Folding a frozen sheet is like folding cardboard.

OUR MOTHER ALWAYS HANGS clothes outside.

No doubt the sun is shining when she pins our jeans and t-shirts on a clothesline that resembles the TV aerial on top of the house. The sunlight, reflecting off the snow, feels like heat in the morning hours. And by nightfall, when the temperature falls to minus twenty-seven Fahrenheit, the clothes are forgotten.

At the end of dinner dishes, after I spit milk-soaked liver into my paper napkin, after the argument with my seventeen-year-old brother who claims he washed dishes yesterday and, besides, has too much homework to dry tonight, after my thirteen-year-old brother wets the corner of a dish towel and snaps it across the back of my thighs—*Stop it, right now!*—I ask Mom where my jeans are.

"Oh," she groans. "I completely forgot. Kerry, go get them. They're outside."

"I'm not going. It's freezing out there. And she's the one who wants them."

"Yours are there too. Now go. Quick, quick."

"What's the rush?" David asks, leaning back on the kitchen stool. His head bangs on the phone. "Are the pants going to walk away?"

"They need to dry before morning," she insists, her mouth tightening.

"Can someone please explain to me why our family can't use a dryer like other families?" Kerry shouts.

"Too much electricity," she says. "Denim takes too long in the machine."

Kerry does as he's told, brings the jeans in under his arm, flat as if a truck has run over them. He leans them against the wall.

"There you go," he says, sweeping his hand towards the row of headless, armless cutout dolls.

We stare at them, transfixed by the improbability of clothes standing alone. How long will it take until the bottoms thaw and the pockets and waistbands and heavy white-crusted zippers topple the pants over?

My brothers and I watch the jeans soften. David makes a gun with his hand. Shoots them as they fall.

I reach for the Wranglers with the perfectly faded knees.

"Oh, no you don't," Kerry says. "Those belong to me."

"Yeah, and leave mine alone too," says David.

For this one brief year when my brothers and I wear the same size, I sneak jeans out of their closet or pull them from their final drying phase, pinned on a line strung behind the furnace.

"The laundry room was dark," I offer as an excuse when caught.

I can still see David coming up the alley with shoulders hunched against a cold wind, the ribbing of white socks glaring under the short jeans he was left with that morning. I look down. I am wearing his pants—too long and a little frayed at the bottom.

IT IS DIANE WHO tells me where the journals are.

Coiled exercise books, scribblers, small notebooks.

David's reflections, his memories.

"Some of them are disturbing," my sister warns.

"They're diaries," I say. "It's the place we put our disturbing thoughts."

I open them greedily, barely giving a thought to his right to privacy. I read and read, taking short breaths, getting impatient when I can't separate the swollen pages easily with my fingertips. David writes like he talks. In long rambling essays or brief sentences of insight he explores the requirements of society versus the needs of the individual. Suburbia kills the soul. Desk jobs kill the body. Parental love has too many expectations for the child. There is half a journal dedicated to God and the Universe. He believes the answer to our spiritual questions lies in science, logic, and the strength of the intellect and will. The word *freedom* is repeated like a mantra. It is his touchstone.

The real momentum of David's writing though comes from his need to clarify and justify the strong feelings that have gripped him. I see him struggling with language and reason, trying to dig deeper and unearth something meaningful: *Among the phalanx, voices of doom rise . . . garbled and misunderstood they, too, are carried over the cliff....* But he ends up rambling, going in circles, unable to punch through to the truth that is eluding him. Often, the entries stop abruptly, like someone has wrenched the writing implement out of his hand and said, *Enough.*

The wooden floorboards above my head groan. One of my parents is up, probably my mother. I listen for a sound on the basement stairs, ready to pounce to the door and turn the lock, but instead I hear the toilet flush. The water sluices down a pipe behind the walls. My nervousness surprises me. I am hiding David's journals as if reading them is a guilty pleasure but it is more like an obsession getting out of control. I can almost hear my mother admonishing me. *They're not ours to read. Sometimes it's better not to know.*

Nothing, black, then darkness. A gathering glow slowly intensifying until it outshines all else. A vision, an illusion, a dream? Nonetheless reality, reality that defies understanding. Exploring, searching, thinking until reaching that vast area of darkness. That unknown that lies beyond. Standing, staring into a void, crestfallen, frustrated, resigned. Air, then ground, then...? Then...we don't have a word for it (not a proper one anyway). It refuses to reveal itself, unless, unless, we take that step, that one small insignificant step we all fear to tread. Standing on the threshold. The ledge is now, the past never was, the future? A deep breath and a step and there is no return.

The dark mystery of death. The unknown.

The last adventure that is the same for all of us, even for those who don't willingly step off their front porches.

...there is another kind of traveller to these far-off lands and though they are lumped in with the others, I know they exist, for I have met

one. They are finished, of that there can be no doubt. They become frustrated and tired and maybe even a little unhappy. But they are not desperate, and with little emotion, they cast it all off like old socks. Cold and rational, with no alternate answer waiting for them, they take the next logical step. The rational extension of all they have believed in. They are brave explorers, these truth seekers.

Don't misunderstand, I don't want to join them on their journey. But still, like a well wisher on a train platform seeing someone off, I understand their need to go. I've convinced myself I am happiest here, there's still so much to do. But maybe at a later time I'll follow of my own choosing.

These must be the pages that Diane is referring to. The coolness that David ascribes to the act of suicide. The postponement of his own death until he is more unhappy. How rational. Yet there is no thought for anyone else who might be hurt by such a death. I find this odd. David's best friend, Todd, killed himself while David was living in Japan. My brother was devastated and yet here on these pages he seems to be making a case (*and I have met one*) for Todd's supposed emotionless exit.

For the next two pages in the journal, David writes almost lightly about how to kill oneself. *Painless is the most popular criteria.* He considers the benefits of the spectacular death, perhaps a front-page story with all of the messiness. He discusses speeding cars, or buses and trains that leave nothing to chance. The high-rise building, a dive into air, is a suitable choice for the ... *publicity seeker or those crushed romantics trying to punish others for their own shortcomings.*

There is one other kind of suicide he describes.

Others like the mystery of going "without a trace." Just slip over the side into the deep water and the death will live long after you're dead.

Most of David's journals contain lengthy examinations on what defines a worthy existence. We are given life. How should it be lived? How should it end? He argues that a free individual must determine both. And so, if the romantic quest is a seeking for an enrichment of life must it also, by its nature, seek death?

David is in his mid-twenties when he fills these books. Tearing a page from Thoreau's journal, he believes that we can live in fear and die, or we can live a life on the edge, and still die. Death is a danger for all of us. My brother never considers any middle ground: the place where a man might give up his aspirations to make someone else happy, or comfortable, or safe. The middle ground of love.

"I HAD A DREAM about David last night," my mother says to me in the morning. "We walked together in the mountains. In Banff."

I see them meandering along the edge of a cliff. Clouds sweep over the icy peaks in long strands. They are heading for a lone hoodoo, a standing, helmeted sentinel of rock perched on a bluff over the Bow River. Snow is falling in the air. They are talking and laughing. The wind erodes their words like sand.

"I woke feeling happy," she says. "Like I was immersed in a warm bath." A look of peace settles on her face.

"I wish I had asked him though," she continues. "I wish I had asked him what happened to him and Sarah. Out on the ocean."

"What would you have wanted to hear?" I prod.

She shakes her head.

What kind of death?

What kind of life?

A TRAGEDY IN A family can be a diversion from what we don't want to look at—its attraction is heavy, impossible to avoid, and if we're not careful we will shift our gaze for too long from the daily routines, where our real lives exist.

I return home to Calgary and find I belong nowhere. My house in the city is the place where I wait. At the hotel, I am neither paying guest or paid employee—just a stranger who wanders. When I look to the mountains and the prairie on the edge of the foothills, the geography offers no connection to what I am feeling. Only the sea would mimic my detachment.

At the end of the day, when no one is sleeping in the darkness of night, a voice whispers: *Who is dead, where are the bodies? Show me the injuries that cause the suffering.*

Sam and I have a mute fight on a Friday night.

I arrive in a loaded station wagon with the kids and come in the back door. He doesn't say hello, doesn't kiss me, but walks right by on the way to the car. "Where's the paper?"

I wince. I can see the boxes in the front hallway.

"Shit," he shouts. "One thing, Cathy. You just had to remember one thing." He turns away and retreats to the office without a bag of our luggage in his hand.

I'm having trouble remembering things, I want to shout after him. *But look, I brought your children. I didn't forget them.*

I muffle my rage because I have no choice. There are guests mulling about in the hallways and I cannot vent my anger here. I hit the swinging door with my shoulder and drag the bags across the library floor and up the stairs.

Five minutes later, I pass Sam in the hallway as I head for the front door.

"You know," he says. "Things have been just crazy around here."

I do know. I can see it. The aging hotel needs attention. The quirky staff requires constant supervision. The guests demand to be attended to. But I am no longer interested. My days in the city are spent dragging the kids from one activity to the next, from breakfast to bed. In the kid-free hours I am doing housework or planning the redecorating. I make lists of the things I am supposed to bring up to the lodge: fabric bolts, carpet samples, office supplies; snowsuits, hats, mittens; changes of clothes, books, toys. But the lists disappear in the growing disorder of the house. My brother is fading from my mind and I struggle to keep him close by. I try to revive him at night with the open maps. Take me with you, I say. Don't leave me here with the walls closing in.

"I'm not your delivery wife," I mutter. I push the heavy door open into a brisk wind coming down from the glacier.

Spring comes late in the mountains, slowly stirring from a deep and frigid sleep. The thaw is unhurried like a hibernating bear waking to consciousness, the space between breaths becoming shorter.

I follow a line of footprints that leads to a trailhead. My steps sink into the oval depressions and I match the stride of a stranger who has set out before me. The route crosses a snow-covered meadow and a footbridge, then narrows to a shoulder-width path. Trees and shrubs crowd the lake's edge, bushes with wrinkled, plum-coloured berries brush against my arm. Winter is retreating along this portion of the trail. My boots leave imprints of octagon shapes in patches of muddy ooze. Thick twisted tree roots escape like brown snakes out of the snow. Even the shoreline is softening, the ice pulling back.

Along the edge of the lake, the ice is thin as glass and opaque as smoke. Across its surface, stars, flowers and tiny sea creatures are spun and hooked like Portuguese lace. I place my finger over a sea urchin and melt it with a brief tap. The image is gone, a single drop of water remains in the still air.

The quiet is broken by a low-note moan echoing across the lake. My throat clenches with fear. Is it a bear on the path, staggering down the mountain, barely awake but hungry? I hear the sound again, but this time it's followed by a loud crack, like a tree has broken in two. It's not an animal. It's the ice. Splitting and cracking, the crystals coming apart. Wounded, the ice cries out.

I step onto the smooth surface and make a row of crushed half-moons. Then I smash the winter lake open with my heel. Again and again. The ice must return to water. This frozen world must be made alive again.

In wet boots, I get back on the trail and follow it to a mountain slope of crumbled rock angling upward like a giant amphitheatre. Boulders brought down by rockslides litter the shoreline. I listen for the sound of someone walking up the riverbed, the crunch of steps, a whistle in the cold air—where is the stranger who set out before me?

Only a kilometre from here is the source of the Bow River. It begins in a plain of ice, a glacier, 7,500 feet above sea level. Under a warm sun a hidden stream, no bigger than the width of a hand, wends its secret way. First an invisible tear, then a seam ripping in two directions. The ancient ice splits and opens like a scar the colour of water.

I remember the glow on David's face when he stared down a crevasse cut into a glacier. That moment is connected to this one, to this bright chill in my heart, to that fear I knew when I was thirteen and I looked into an ice abyss.

I won't fall.

I think of what remains of David and Sarah. Floating until the flesh is pierced and torn. Sea creatures feeding on them.

It will take time for the bodies to sink to the ocean floor and more time for silt and sand to cover the ragged forms in the darkness. Bones will dissolve. Minerals will seep in. Eventually, they will be as rock—fossilized changelings. The earth will have to shift into a new geological era before David and Sarah are visible to the light once more.

A train whistle echoes across the valley. A lingering lament, the faint sound carried along the rock walls. Yet there are no tracks near here, not for thirty miles. I look to see if I'm mistaken—perhaps it's a car horn in the parking lot—and I see Num-ti-Jah. Scrawny pine trees screen most of the two-storey building, but the historic red roof floats against a backdrop of mountain and sky. It looks like it belongs in a German fairy tale. Sam has chosen such a strange place to satisfy his yearnings.

I turn back and head for the hotel. I walk in soft grey light. The day is falling, burdened with dusk.

I wonder how long it will it take for the thaw to be complete?

How long until we emerge from winter, the lightless edge of grief?

And what will remain?

CASTLETOWNBERE

To face the elements is, to be sure, no light matter
when the sea is in its grandest mood. You must then know
the sea, and know that you know it, and not forget
that it was made to be sailed over.

JOSHUA SLOCUM

MACCARTHY'S PUB IS DARK except for an errant ray of sunshine piercing the window that faces the town square. The beam sets the bar on fire, the polished wood glows amber under a set of hands gripping a glass.

"Good morning," I say to Adrienne MacCarthy, the owner of this bar. "Morning," I mumble to the man facing her. I slide onto a stool next to his. The place is almost empty, one couple and some singles sit at the small round tables in the back.

"It is a fine *afternoon*," she says. "Not a cloud in the sky."

"It doesn't feel like an Irish day ought to. I expected more grey in this country."

"We're not like the rest of Ireland, you know. We have sun and palm trees." She smiles.

"Just like the Caribbean." It feels good to laugh.

Adrienne puts a pint of golden liquid in front of me.

"Hair of the dog?" I ask.

"Cheers, luv." She turns to the man sitting beside me. "You all right, sir?"

A wave of his hand indicates he's done. He pours the last inch of beer down his throat, slams the pint down on the bar and turns to me. "It's a damn shame, Miss," he says. "A damn shame." His voice is a river tumbling over the rocks. "My father used to say one thing about the sea. *She takes what she needs.*"

He pushes some bills across the counter and tips his head towards my glass. Giving me a nod he slides out the red painted door like a shadow erased by light.

"They know who you are, what you're doing here," Adrienne says, while tucking the money into the drawer of an old-fashioned cash register.

"I guess the story's spreading."

"It's Ireland. It'll travel up the whole peninsula by tomorrow."

"Well, that's good. Maybe someone will remember something." I glance towards the window, bright with light—it reminds me of sitting in a dark theatre, waiting for a film to begin.

I've come to Castletownbere eleven months after David and Sarah sailed from this fishing town. From here I will continue on to Mull where Sarah's family is gathering for a remembrance. Heather invited our entire family but I will be the only one there. Sam couldn't leave the hotel so he and a couple of babysitters are taking care of the children. My sister can't travel because of Mark. Kerry showed no interest and though my father wanted to come he wouldn't leave my mother alone. I don't think she needed to see where her son had lived.

Someone asked me in the bar last night if it was hard to be here, knowing this was the last place David had been. Yes, I answered. I see my brother's reddish hair disappear around every corner.

"WHERE IS THE LAST area you can pinpoint the *Mugwump*?" the interviewer for Cork Radio FM asks me. I hear the question through the handset of a white rotary-dial phone while sitting in a small tidy lounge room. I am doing the interview in the coastal town of Allihies, on the western end of the Beara Peninsula.

"You mean on the ocean, itself?"

"Right."

"Three miles southwest of Mizen Head peninsula. They left Castletownbere the evening of August thirty-first. They made a radio broadcast to the coastguard on Valencia Island the following day. And then there's nothing."

"No further radio communications or sightings since that date?"

"No."

"So, what do you hope to achieve with your visit to Castletownbere?" This is the real question, the one I've asked myself every hour since arriving in this town.

I stare at a row of tiny china figurines sitting dustless on a sill. White lace curtains hang on the lower half of the window. "I'd like to learn something about the boat. Or Sarah and David. Our families have nothing, you know. No bodies. Nothing to tell us what happened. So, I'm asking questions

around town and down at the docks. I'm hoping to find someone who may have talked to them about their voyage. A
conversation in a bar or on the pier. Maybe someone came
aboard the boat."

"Right. And I presume at this stage that you actually have
given up hope of ever seeing David and Sarah again?"

"Yes, we have. It's been eleven months."

"Before you go home, is there something you are expecting to hear? Is there something that will help?"

"I guess I'd like to hear that *Mugwump* was in good shape
and so was the crew."

I'd like to know if things could have been different.

After the interview I hang up the phone and go out onto to
the street.

People are leaning against their doorways. Heads lowered,
chins to chests, but the eyes are not fixed on their feet. They
are watching a funeral procession make its way to the cemetery.

As the mourners pass I consider the interviewer's question.
What might I expect to hear from someone who was on the
boat? How a dockhand thought *Mugwump* was sitting too low
in the water? A discussion about a leak followed, but David was
sure the problem was corrected? Would I want to hear that
Sarah disagreed with David? That she believed the forecast of
bad weather could be a problem for *Mugwump*?

We can't wait any longer, Sarah. We're already behind schedule.

But a day or two won't make a difference, David.

The hell with the weather! His trademark impatience. *It'll
never be perfect, Sarah. We've got to go now or it won't happen.*

"Ninety-one," says a man stopping beside me. He takes off
his cap and runs pale fingers through cobwebs of hair. "She was

born here in Allihies. Never went anywhere. Seven children, or was it eight to begin with? Ah, God bless her. A good long life."

I nod at the man.

The cemetery is on a hill. The coffin is carried through an open metal gate into a graveyard ringed with a rock wall as old as the three hundred-year-old tombstones inside. It would be a fine place to be buried—a view to the sea. I remember my grandfather wanting a plot close to the Red River in Winnipeg. *So I can look out over the water,* he explained to my mother. He lived to a hundred and one.

I put my hand on the wall. Green moss flows out of the cracks, soft and molten. Only a thin layer of dirt supports this growth.

Earth to earth, the burial prayer states. Ashes. Dust. No mention of the sea.

The Irish have stories to explain why some family plots are empty. Their literature is filled with legends of lost, beleaguered mariners. Men who go *away*—missing in this world but alive in another. Often sailors are saved from unmerciful storms by some offered grace. A woman, standing on the shore of an enchanted island, calls across the water. Perched on the ship's bow, the captain searches the fog and sees a ball of thread thrown through the haze. The clew fixes to his palm and the ship is pulled to land.

In other tales, sailors sail forever. An island rises out of the sea, mist hanging between the gunwales and shore like a thick grey cloak, but no matter how the men reach for it they can never narrow the space. The island always drifts away.

What do you hope to achieve with your visit to Castletownbere?
Perhaps just one thing. To carry this story.
The telling is the liturgy.

"IT'S ROMANTIC, ISN'T IT?" a young woman says as she pulls up a stool next to mine. Her blue eyes are sparkling. "A man and a woman on the sea like that, just the two of them."

"I guess it is," I say. The myth of the exiled couple captures the listener, old narratives still resonating in modern times. If only the endings were different: Romeo and Juliet escape Verona together; Abelard lives in shame and humiliation but together with the beloved Heloise; Tristan and his Irish Isolde, bound forever by a love potion, marry and unite in life as well as death. But we are moved more because of the tragedy, the love that was never fully realized.

"Sailin' for an island. *Madeira*. I can just see it in me mind," she says tucking a strand of long brown hair behind her ear. "It makes me want to cry."

"Another round?" Adrienne interupts.

"And such a little boat, I heard," the young woman continues. "So small for such a storm. If it was a storm...."

"Yes, *Mugwump* was small," I agree, taking a sip of a fresh beer. I am caught in the tale again, repeating all the details and the unsubstantiated particulars I've come to believe in. "But she was sturdy. Previous owners sailed her to the Caribbean."

"Sarah must have really loved your brother." The young blue eyes are watering. "You know, to go with him."

"Oh, I think she wanted to sail as badly as David," I counter. "She was every bit the adventurer he was." But as soon as I say it, I'm uncertain of the truth of this statement. Sarah was certainly more daring than me but have I made her into some iconic figure of female bravery? I want to believe that Sarah was not following my brother's dream, but that the sea called to her, too, and she answered with her own courage and imagination. I want Sarah to have found meaning for her life in the tasks and trials of sailing, as well as love.

I look at the woman's unlined face. "She was beautiful and only thirty-four," I tell her, almost feeling guilty. As we all know, to die young and beautiful is double the tragedy.

Adrienne pours me another and won't take my money. "You've had a loss, girl," she says. "You're mourning. It's the least we can do here. Come, there's a few people here I want you to meet.

"This is the Canadian woman who lost her brother," she says to a table filled with locals at the back of the pub. "You've heard the story? Cathy's looking for information."

Most have something to say:

—It was a bold adventure. You've got to admire that—

—Wish I could tell you I'd seen the little yacht—

—I heard she was a pretty thing. Mahogany inside? Beautiful—

—Red sails, you say—

—It's a sad thing, isn't it?—

"They know what you're feeling," she says, later, when I express surprise at how easily the townspeople share their own stories—grandfathers, nephews, husbands, who have drowned or gone missing. "There isn't a family in town that hasn't lost someone out there." She tilts her blond head in the direction of the docks.

It hasn't been like this at home. So many haven't known what to say.

My mother has suffered the most. So few of her friends have been able to speak to her about David. At first, she thought they were waiting for our family to announce that we no longer hoped for his and Sarah's survival. But when that day came, all she was offered were reluctant murmurs of sympathy.

Sadly, what our friends and even family members do not realize is that a hole has opened in us, an absence that aches all the more because there is no feeling, only numbness, coldness, and little understanding. A voice echoes inside, repeating the words, *gone gone gone.* What we see in our minds we try to grasp—something heavy falling through the water, a body, a heart, or was it just a pebble that slipped through our fingers into the dark? What we need to hear are certain words: *I am sorry for your emptiness.*

For our family, missing is a perpetual state of wondering. Missing is the unfinished story seeking an ending that can only be found in the imagination.

IRISH BEER FEEDS MELANCHOLY and strange dreams.

The Old Convent Hostel is cold and damp. Even with the crucifixes removed and the walls freshly painted, the room still feels like a stripped-down cell. Outside the door, the hallway echoes with sounds of measured footfalls.

I dream of David and me, walking side by side in the narrow alley of a Mediterranean village. The sun is so bright I must shield my eyes. I can't see my brother's face but I hear the voice, deep and resonating from behind the prominent apple caught in his throat.

I want to ask him: *What happened? Where is Sarah? What's on the other side?* But I stop myself. What if David thinks he is sleeping and dreaming? What if he doesn't know he has left this world?

We are not alone as we follow the worn stone road under our feet. There are others, strangers wandering like us, bodies moving past each other, yet no one touching. We seem to be part of a throng like pilgrims at Easter. The living and the dead, dreaming and mourning for each other.

When I turn to David to see if his face has changed, we are forced apart by a bull that has entered the street running wildly. We flatten ourselves against opposite walls and watch the beast swing its head back and forth, the neck pivoting in anger. The bull charges up and down in quick bursts of fury, stopping, searching, pawing at the stone. Its hide glows brilliant white like steel heated in a forge. When a woman in the crowd tries to run, the bull knocks her to the ground and holds her with its blackened hooves. The horns dig into her flesh. There is no blood, only the twist of opposing moons in the yielding skin.

When I wake I can't remember a single word David has said. Even in dreams, the dead keep the truth to themselves.

IT IS ALMOST NOON in Castletownbere.

The streets are empty as though all the townspeople were up late last night and are reluctant to rise. Blue and yellow row houses stand quiet. Lace-curtained windows are closed and dark. I walk along Main Street, taking deep breaths with each step. A faint shudder runs under my skin like a feeling of expectation. I am sure I will hear something today.

The town square is ablaze with colour. Flower boxes filled with bright blooms spill over the windowsills. Red and purple. Pink. Zinnias and petunias. A netting of mauve lobelia trailing to the ground. I wonder if David put his nose to the blossoms last August, recalling the geraniums and marigolds of our mother's small garden under the clothesline? Did he turn and admire, too, the forested green and blue slopes that rise behind the town? The Sliabh Miskish and Caha Mountains are similar to the hills of Scotland. Sarah must have noticed this. Did she look to the sky above them, see a gathering of white clouds and make a wish for fair winds?

I make my way down to the harbour. The dark clouds of the morning, puckered like taffeta, have been ripped open and a dome of brilliant blue arches overhead. Gulls are circling a point in the sky. Perhaps a fishing vessel is on its way in. Alongside the quay, the sea is grey and slick. It slops sluggishly against the painted fishing trawlers. The brightly coloured hulls, mirrored in the water, create the illusion that I am entering a port in the southern latitudes.

Before I came to Ireland, I imagined the recollections I might find here: David and Sarah drinking in a pub; David juggling for kids on the docks; a local sailor invited on board to see *Mugwump's* classic wooden interior. But instead, the details are spare.

According to a member of the Irish Marine Emergency Service, when *Mugwump* first arrived, David and Sarah tied up to the quay, filled the boat's water stores, and then moved anchorage to a buoy. A day and half later they departed in the late evening.

"It was a peaceful night," the man says. "Calm. After that, the clouds rolled in again."

In Limar's, an old-fashioned chandlery with worn wooden floors, and ropes and buoys hanging from the walls, a woman remembers David and Sarah coming in.

"He was a friendly lad, real excited about this adventure. You know, jovial. He had a big laugh."

I smile at her description of his personality. "His voice could really boom sometimes."

"His girlfriend was quiet." Yes, Sarah would have hung back, unless there was something she needed to know.

The woman shakes her hair and re-knots her pony tail. "I liked them. They looked happy."

I plead for more detail. Clothing, bits of conversation, an attitude. I want to see them, hear them. Did David have a beard? *No, I don't think so.* Was Sarah's hair short or long? *Shoulder length.* Did they say anything about the boat? A shake of the head.

Chance encounters with strangers leave little residue.

I find the harbourmaster in the second-floor office of a pale yellow building on the wharf. He's sitting behind his desk wearing a blue jean jacket. His hands barely reach the desktop. A four-foot girth keeps him leaning back in his chair. When I introduce myself, he says, "I'm really sorry, Miss. These things are never easy."

Captain Bill Jones recalls the weather on the evening they left. "It was a clear night. First one in a week. I saw them leave at about eleven at night." He twists his shoulders as if trying to shake off something irritating, an insect or a scratchy tag under his shirt. "They said they were headed for Madeira, non-stop. Though I didn't talk to them about it, they certainly would have heard the weather broadcasts. Another cold front was crossing the Atlantic and that night, August thirty-first, was a window. They probably thought they'd get away from land and be ahead of the bad weather."

He pauses, rolls his lips, and looks out the window towards the harbour. I follow his stare. The blue pieces of sky are being swallowed. Clouds smooth as Egyptian cotton are rolling in again. It will certainly rain by tonight.

I want to ask him if there's anything he remembers about their faces—a look of doubt, fear, worry, even overconfidence; or was there something they said, a comment that would be mean-ingful now considering the circumstances. But it seems so desperate to ask this stranger for a character assessment of two people he met briefly almost a year ago. Have I really travelled all the way from Canada to ask an aging, grey-haired man to look into his memory for a shadow that may have crossed my brother's eyes or to recall some words that would give his and Sarah's death a reason?

I cannot do it. Grief isn't a question with an answer.

Instead I say, "The coastguard told me twenty or more fishermen are lost every year in storms and accidents in Irish and British waters."

"Could be," he grunted. He rolls his lips. "Last week a fishing boat found a skull caught in its nets. There's a woman in town who's sure it's her husband."

I look back to the window. Worn trawlers, painted blue, green, orange with purple trim, are moored next to the processing warehouses. The midship gunnels are low in the water. It would be easy to fall over the side with a beam-on wave.

The captain spreads out a chart covering Cork Harbour to Dingle Bay. "Here's Mizen Head." He points to an area inside the half circle that indicates the lighthouse's arc of visibility. "We know they made it that far."

My eye wanders to the left side of the chart where the sea is divided into two-kilometre squares, numbers indicating depths in metres scattered randomly: 141, 85, 99. A sea floor as varied in geography as land mass. I look closer and see tiny ships scattered next to shorelines.

"Wrecks?" I ask.

"These waters are littered with them, going all the way back to the sixteenth century."

"Do you think they should have left?" I ask. "Knowing the weather would take a turn?"

"Your brother was anxious to go. Maybe in his mind it was now or never."

I have played that scene already in my mind.

"That's exactly what's so troubling," I say. "This idea of now or never. Maybe another time would have meant a different outcome."

"Possibly. Circumstances can change in a day, in a week," the captain says. "And weather reports are not always right. The sea is unpredictable. Lots of things can happen but even with good forecasts, sailing is risky."

Sailing is risky.

Everyone agrees on this point, but why isn't this answer ever enough for me?

Is it because I refuse to accept that my brother was a risk-taker?

Risk-takers aren't careful. They have little fear. They put their own needs first, thinking their lives belong only to themselves.

Risk-takers want to be remembered for their dramatic deaths but don't seem to understand what that means for those who outlive them.

Risk-takers don't weigh the odds. They believe the Gods will step in.

We own our lives, David reminds me. *And our drives.*

But that's not all of it. You owned a piece of mine too.

Without risk, nothing can change.

Living a life of risk is not the same as living a life of freedom.

On the way back to the Old Convent, I see a poster of my sunglass-clad brother and Sarah taped on the door of Murphy's SuperValu Store. *M I S S I N G* is typed across the top. I mailed a stack of these to the Police Station last October.

"Ah, never heard from them?" Mr. Murphy says, shaking his head. "It's mighty queer. They were keen to get goin', tired of waitin' for good weather," the storeowner says. "I remember that much. We were chattin' while I rang in their groceries. I remember they bought bananas."

"Bananas?" I repeat.

"They wanted fresh fruit for the first few days."

Bananas would have been a luxury at sea. Yellow peels dropped into water the colour of steel.

THE HOUSE SITS ON top of a hill two miles east of Castletownbere.

From the yard there is a panoramic view of the waters of Bantry Bay. The sea glitters in the morning light, gleaming silver like sharpened blade tips. I follow a gravel path around to the back of the house where a woman named Ellen is waiting for me. She leads me under an iron arch overgrown with tangled vine and into a lush blooming garden. Across the expanse of grass I see where a second archway opens to more botanical riches. I feel like a shrunken Alice.

"Take whatever you want," she says, giving me a basket and some cutting shears. She turns and walks back into the house, leaving me in the middle of a small sub-tropical paradise, warmed by the vigorous Gulf Stream.

I stand among the rhododendrons, giant pink heads and glossy leaves, and admire the beds that wind around a lawn of deep green. I am here because Ellen's daughter said something to me in the bar last night: "There should be flowers for the dead, Cathy. Go up the hill and see my mother."

Choosing flowers is one of the mourning rituals. But what kind of flowers? These are not to adorn a church. They will be thrown into a grave of water. Should I begin with an oriental poppy with scarlet paper petals, the sad bloom harvested for sleep and dreams? Or, perhaps a branch of pink bleeding hearts, hanging like medals earned in war? But then I see the lilies—growing in clustered bouquets of reds and yellows, a dozen flowers on each stalk. I would love to cut the stems at the ground and carry away a hundred scented blossoms: tigers with freckled petals curling away from the centre; white pendulous trumpets, blooms angled downward like the head of a shy girl. When I pull a stem towards me, driving the shears low on the stalk, pollen falls to my arm leaving a stain the colour of saffron.

The daisies are growing like weeds so I cut the shastas happily, clipping close to the earth, trimming away the leaves until my fist is holding a nosegay. I move on to a clump of orange gloriosas, erect like sunflowers, and then to the purple johnny-jump-ups peeking out from under the shadows. I pick the tiny blooms with fairy faces. Their stems are short. They will be the first to loosen and fly towards the sea.

The basket is soon overflowing. Graceful blue columbines dangle over the woven edge, poisonous crimson foxgloves droop next to long stalks of yellow snapdragons—I could not resist the yellow mandibles. David and I used to chase each other with the mouths snapping.

What now? More scent. Follow the bees.

Lavender is spiking purplish blooms at the back of the garden. Next to it are the scarlet flowers of bee balm. The scent of mint permeates my fingertips as I cut a square-edged stalk. Growing along the garden's edge is rosemary, a traditional funeral herb to help mourners remember: the initial burst of lemon wakes the senses, then comes the lingering pine scent—a walk through the quiet forests of the past. What is it we are to remember? How we once loved the dead? How we must not yield to the dark waves of forgetting? Ophelia said to her brother Laertes: *There's rosemary, that's for remembrance—pray you, love, remember.*

I tear a long strand of ivy from the iron archway and wrap the vine around the stems like a green ribbon. This might hold the bouquet together for its long fall.

MIZEN HEAD IS A promontory of land with seven-hundred-foot cliffs edging the most southerly point of mainland Ireland. The signal station sits on Cloghane Island, a small rocky bit of land that juts into the swirling Atlantic tides. To reach the island I walk the ninety-nine steps leading to an arched bridge that spans a deep gorge. The bridge shudders as I cross, the sea roiling below. I cling to the railing and hold the basket of flowers close to my chest.

From the old lighthouse I fight the wind down a path to a viewpoint. Sheer drop-offs, hundreds of feet down, fall away on three sides. I grip the railing tightly while the wind slams my body with erratic blows. My hair is in my mouth. My jacket might be tearing. I must hold on like I'm on a roller coaster. But the view is worth it. Glittering in the sunlight, bulging like an opal stone set in a ring, the ocean is a cut gem of iridescent blue and green. This is the beauty that calls to sailors.

I wonder how *Mugwump* would have looked from here. Flying under a blue sky would she be just a flash of colour on the water? Or a small triangle spied by a dreamy boy standing on this rocky edge? *Oh, Daddy, look!* the child shouts into the wind. *A boat!* The father sees it too. *A good day for a sail,* he says, keeping a firm hold of his son's jacket. *Not a cloud in the sky.*

To the southeast, I can just make out Fastnet Rock. The famous pinnacles of shale, known commonly as "The Teardrop of Ireland," are only a dark blur on the water's surface. Carraig Aonar is its real name—The Lonely Rock. An island veiled by sheets of white spray. I have read that the waters around Fastnet are some of the most turbulent in the Atlantic. The prevailing wind is from the northwest. The North Atlantic Current slides north and east along the coastlines. The place is a spinning magnet of wind and sea currents.

The flowers cannot be thrown from this place. The blooms will fly back at me instead of falling down to the sea.

I return to the arched bridge. The sea is churning in the narrow channel far below my feet. Scattered spray fans the cliff walls.

The wind tugs impatiently at the flowers in my arms so I let them go.

The bouquet opens like a spring garden. Stems and blossoms coming free. Flowers tumbling, one by one by one, disappearing into white mist.

"I wish you fair winds and a following sea."

A man standing at the other end of the bridge clasps his hands together, prayer-like, and leans over the railing. A camera dangles from his neck. His reddish hair catches the sunlight. David was afraid of heights but he would have looked down, anyway.

"I DIDN'T THINK YOU were coming in," says Adrienne, glancing at the clock. The hands hover over the number eleven.

It's a quiet night at MacCarthy's. A couple of tables are filled, one man at the bar. I sit down next to him and rest my arms against the curved bull nose edge. The counter is sticky. I'm getting used to being glued to this long plank of wood.

"How was Mizen Head?" she asks.

"Windy," I answer. I rub my forehead. My temples feel hot. Like a skull left in the fire.

"Headache?"

"I wish it would just fall off."

"Drink?"

"One beer, please. Don't let me have more."

Adrienne smiles. "Okay." She draws a draught and puts it in front of me. The stout is warm as it passes over my lips, soft as cream. I place the glass on the bar and turn it clockwise in my hand. The foam makes slow swirls.

"I want to thank you, Adrienne. For everything you've done for me." For the last five days, this woman has kept me fed and mildly drunk.

"It's too bad I never got the chance to meet your brother. I'm sure I would've liked him. And Sarah too."

"Did I mention his temper?"

"I think the Irish respect this characteristic."

Adrienne picks up a cloth and crumples it under her left palm. She wipes the counter with an absent gesture, her hand sliding back and forth though nothing has spilled. "I think it's hard to believe in death when there are no bodies. In a way, David and Sarah are still out there, sailing on a long voyage."

Still sailing. *Away.* A story with no ending.

I play with my glass, turning it around faster and faster.

The way you live your life, you're risking your present.

The beer is sloshing up the sides, the froth thick and white.

The way I live mine, I'm risking my future.

A sharp pain knifes me in the centre of my forehead and the glass slips out of my hand. It rolls to the floor and shatters.

But I'm the one who still has time.

"Stay where you are," Adrienne says, coming around from behind the bar. "I'll take care of it."

She picks up the largest shards, places them carefully in her hand and then sweeps the floor with a short broom. When she's finished Adrienne gives my shoulder a small shake. Tears are streaming down my face as if a broken beer glass in an Irish pub is the saddest thing I've ever seen.

IN MY ROOM AT the Old Convent, I sit at a small writing desk. I imagine *Mugwump* in full sail. A northwesterly is blowing, white caps fleck across the water's surface like points of light. As she recedes, the angles of the sails soften until the yacht is a small sun slipping over the horizon, red and on fire. When she is almost gone I take my pen and hold it over a pad of narrow lined paper. I will pick up the threads of the story, tie a knot, and hold *Mugwump* back for another moment.

What will I write? A ship ramming the hull? A container floating just under the surface, murderously slicing her open? A rogue wave crashing, beam-on? Or will it be the quick hand of accident, not fate, a human error that is the cause—a sliding foot, a failure by David or Sarah to close their palms around something solid, and one or both spilling into the sea through inattention?

We are tossed on an ocean of absolute blackness.

There is no up and down. No horizon. No domed sky above. Even the boat has joined the dark void. We cannot see her deck or mast in the shadowy gloom. The sail is gone too.

Out of the water, a gathering glow slowly intensifies until it out-shines all else. A vision? An illusion? Or the unknown that lies beyond? Standing on the threshold, the ledge is now. The past never was, the future is only a dream. A deep breath and a step and there is no looking back.

Isle of Mull

Every human,
every mortal one
meets within the compass of his voyage
Troy upon Troy upon Troy,
victories, failures, never-ending siege...
but whatever be the outcome of his strivings
always and urgent is the strive within him
to steer at last on a course to Ithaca,
his place unique,

John Kincaid

The Caledonian MacBrayne ferry, *Isle of Mull*, is vibrating alongside the cement pier extending into the harbour at Craignure.

David swings my backpack onto my shoulders. I wince under the weight.

"Is it really necessary to take all those rocks and shells home?" he asks.

"Actually, it's only half of what I scavenged. I've left the rest for you."

"Gee, thanks."

"You're welcome."

David hugs me for a second time. "Thank you for coming, Cath. It was so great to be able to show you Mull."

"It was good, wasn't it?"

"And maybe next time we meet, there'll be palm trees and sand."

"Spain?"

"You never know."

"Keep in touch and let me know how the boat search goes."

"OK."

"See you."

I hug him, kiss his cheek, then make my way up the ramp.

When I get to the top level, I scan the pier. He sees me first and yells my name. I find him below, grinning and swinging both arms. He raises a hand and pretends to have a lit lighter. I laugh through a film of tears.

The ferry departs, churning across the Firth of Lorne towards Oban, but David remains, waving until his grey sweater merges with the sea.

Three-and-a-half years later, I walk down the same ferry ramp and buy a bus ticket for Fionnphort.

I remember it all, the twists of the single-track road, lanes veering off, lay-bys every hundred yards. The island is greener in the summer months, a dozen different shades painted across the fields and hills, a deep canvas of broad and light strokes. The gullies are thick with ferns. The spruce trees are dark and tall. In the month of July, there is purple heather too.

The bus follows the route I know: Kinloch, Pennyghael, Bunessan. I ask the driver to drop me at the end of the road that leads to Bruach Mhor, Heather and her partner Derek's home. The little white house with the grey shale roof sits on a hill.

I walk up the gravel lane around to the backyard. David and Sarah's blue and white caravan is still here, the fibreglass awning casting a yellow glow over the doorway. The small stone patio David built with granite slabs from the nearby quarry has moss growing in the spaces like mortar. I kneel down and touch the green with my fingertips.

Houdini, Sarah and David's cat, comes up behind me and rubs his head on my leg.

"I CAN'T BELIEVE YOU live on a Scottish island, David." I shake my head while I pull my backpack out of Myrtle the Turtle's trunk. "Life has certainly changed from suburban Winnipeg."

"And I can't believe you've really come."

For the next two weeks, David and I talk like we've met for the first time in our lives. We have the odd, sudden intimacy that travellers share when they meet another national in a foreign land. We trade travel stories and speak of the world in its capacity to create wonder. Like him, I love the silver skies and cool winds of Mull. The island calms me, as does my brother's voice. Something has changed in him. He is quieter, more content.

David tells me stories about the people who live here. He asks about my life and listens. Because so much of our adult relationship has been spent on the phone or through letters, we relish being able to converse in person. Sometimes, we talk about our childhoods. At our ages, thirty-six and not yet thirty-four, the shared history has become comforting and sat-isfying. We seem to know who we are when together. The afternoons we go walking are some of the finest days on Mull. We head across the fields and moors just to wander. We climb rocky hills that look over a tumbling sea—its ancient voice ris-ing up to us.

Mull is a place for David to think in, to be himself. The same is true for me.

"OH, YOU'VE ARRIVED." A woman's voice sings out behind me.

"Yes, I'm here, Heather." My voice startles Houdini and he runs under the caravan.

"I didn't see the bus drop you." She gives me a long embrace. "Come, into the house." I leave my bag in the yard and follow her into a cool kitchen with white-plastered walls. Along one wall, open shelves hold Shakespeare, Keats, Robbie Burns as well as dishes, mugs, and serving platters. Heather takes a cup down and pours tea. A small rainbow flickers across the surface. I pour milk into the blackness but it barely lightens.

"Your trip all right?" Heather asks. "You made all the right connections in Glasgow and Oban?"

"It was fine. The most exciting part was when the bus had to stop for the cows standing in the middle of the road."

"The *heilan' coos*?" she says in Scottish vernacular.

"Yes. The orange ones with the big horns and long shaggy hair."

David had found their complacency staggering. One day he had marched across the beach at Loch Buie waving his arms at a small herd lying on the sand. "Could someone please explain the purpose of these beasts?" he shouted to the sky.

"I miss Dave," Heather says, lifting the metal-wrapped pot. "We liked him so much. He was part of this family." I know. I had witnessed this. The acceptance of my strong, opinionated brother. Their delight with his presence.

"He was such a nice man to be around. Always so happy, so full of life."

David loved Heather too. His voice softened when he spoke to her, his demeanour calmed. And she was a gentle mother-in-law, not interfering in the couple's life even though they lived in her back yard.

"I am glad you're here, Cathy," Heather says. "I was hoping your parents might come with you but I understand it's a long way for them."

But the reason wasn't the distance. My mother thought that Heather's family celebration to remember David and Sarah's lives would be too sad for her. And my father still seems uncertain about his son's death. "How do we really know for sure?" he had said to me just a month ago.

"I have some photographs of the boat," she says. "I'm not sure what you've seen."

Anchored in the Ross of Mull, *Mugwump* looks like the prize David thought she was—scraped and polished, painted like new. I wonder what Heather thought when she saw it last July? Had she expected something so small?

Heather holds a photo in her hand for a long time. Sarah and David are lying together on a narrow bench below deck. The picture is a little hazy as if the cabin is filling with steam. I can almost smell the damp wood.

"Tea?" Heather offers, putting the picture down face first. Her eyes are blue like her daughter's.

I'm sorry, Heather.

Yes, more tea.

"You'll have the most privacy here," Heather says as she pushes open the little aluminum door, then stands aside to let me enter.

I climb up the metal step, duck my head, and step inside the caravan. The stale air stirs. A mélange of dust, propane, mould, sulphur matches, sea air, damp wool, and an indistinguishable spice. Curry? Are these to be the smells that trigger memories of David?

I take in a breath. Sadness fills my chest like a breaking wave. This is where my brother is missing from.

The caravan still looks inhabited. A tea mug on the counter. The cutlery drawer not completely pushed in. An old issue of *Wooden Boat* is tossed on the table. There is a casual air about the items that remain, as if the occupants have just stepped out the door and planned to return, quite soon.

I open an upper cupboard. Dishes, glasses, mugs. Below the sink, detergent, pots, towels. A lower drawer under the narrow sofa sticks when I tug at it, so I put my hand inside and press down on the soft clothes that prevent it from opening. David's socks, shorts, t-shirts spring free, liberated from their confinement. I lift out his grey sweater and find a set of juggling sacks tucked under the arms. The jester's tools: small, soft-sided balls filled with grain.

At the closet door, I pause. The floor-to-ceiling compartment is the largest storage place in the caravan, just big enough for a small child. It's similar to the one David used for hiding in our family trailer. My thumb pushes down on the square plastic retractor of the handle. I recognize the hardware—the same ones used on a sailing vessel. The door pops open like pressurized air is released. A white sweatshirt slides forward.

I slide the hangers across the wooden dowel. A pair of running pants, two collared shirts, jeans. The jeans almost hang to the floor, the wire distended into a round "O" shape. I slip them off and hold them against me. He grew so much bigger than me. I put them back, next to a sweater drooping at the shoulders like a disconsolate man and leave the door open.

I grab David's juggling balls and go out into the yard. Only half-filled now, the six-sided sacks are soft and loose. A thread hangs from the tiny stitches where a hand has mended the seams. I weigh them in my palm and then throw the sacks into the air. The soft red hearts fall in slow arcs. Fine powder scatters. My open mouth tastes wool dusted with mould and salt.

I miss my brother. I miss his ambition and daring. I miss his judgmental and passionate arguments. I miss his struggles to find meaning and purpose, even when they were dark and hurtful. I miss his laugh. But there is something else I miss even more. I miss being a part of it. I miss being attached to his life.

"How are the children?"

The phone crackles like wrapping paper torn from a gift. I wait for Sam to hear my question.

The satellite phone at Num-ti-Jah has a multi-second delay. In order to have a reasonable conversation the finished speaker has to wait at least three seconds for the beginning of the listener's reply. But it's hard to do. The long silence makes everyone want to interrupt the pause with, *Are you still there?*

"Good. Everybody's fine," Sam says, answering my question.

"Is David taking the . . . ," I begin.

"They seem to like . . . ," Sam interrupts.

". . . medicine for his cough?" I finish the question.

". . . the babysitters." Sam completes his statement and attempts to answer my question with, "What? No, he's finished."

"Shit, I hate this satellite…"

"What?" Sam tries again.

"Happy Birthday."

"… he's still hacking a bit. What?"

"Was there cake?"

"Why?"

"Is it asthma, again? It's your birthday, Sam."

"Tegan's is tomorrow."

Now, nothing is making sense.

"Listen. You talk. I'll wait."

"Tia's great with the kids. I'll take David back to the doctor when I have a chance. The chef is making Tegan a cake."

"O.K. How's the lodge? Is it full? Are you still there?"

"Good. We're at the lodge."

"No, I mean…"

"You know we're at the lodge…"

"I thought we got cut…"

"So, how's Sarah's…?"

"…off."

"…mom?"

"…all right?"

"The kids said to say…."

"I miss…."

"…they miss…."

"…him…."

"…you."

We finally give up. I put the receiver down and kick the screen door open. The late afternoon sun is shining but a breeze with a sharp bite blows across the yard. My skin explodes in goose bumps. *Satellite phone torture* is what that should be called. The conversation was like firing lead pellets at each other. We spoke in fragments, heard the same—words cut in two with our impatient interruptions. All we needed to do was count to three.

"MY GOD, THEY WERE happy to be finally leaving," says Andrew, the fifty-something owner of the Keel Row Bar. His elbows rest on the counter. He looks dreamy or drunk as he pulls a beer, white foam spilling over the glass. The eyelids droop with invisible weights.

"Were they?" I ask.

"I saw them off. Sailed out with them, well ... not with them, I chased them, in fact, in the *Sequina*. They were kind of sneaking off." He laughs. "When I caught up we both dropped anchor. I had some cold beer, so I threw them a couple of cans and we just sat and chatted for a bit."

"So you were the last one from Mull to see them."

"I guess I was. Bless their hearts, for sure." We are silent for a moment. "You know, they should never have sailed up to Mull," sighs Andrew. "They should've left straight from Portsmouth. They sailed all the way up Ireland to here and then had to go all the way back down again."

"Well, David considered it their shakedown cruise. They really hadn't done that much sailing with *Mugwump*."

"What they really wanted was to come up here and see their friends," says Andrew. "Wanted to show the boat off and why not? Have a little chat, like the good old times. Good cracker, that Dave." He laughs loud and then starts to cough and bark.

"Come on," he says, waving me on with one hand, cigarette glowing. "Let's go sit." He comes around from behind the bar. We find a table at the other end of the room near the fireplace.

"What did you think of *Mugwump*, Andrew?"

"It was a lovely boat. Beautiful. I'm sure it must have been capable of sailing round the world. No reason why it shouldn't."

He stubs out his cigarette and lights another. His hands shake with a small tremor. "I was a little concerned about her construction, though."

"Why?" I ask, leaning forward so I can catch every word.

"The hull was fibreglass and the decks were wood. When a boat is made of all one material and joined together along the deck line it's just stronger. I think the coach house might have been a problem too. It had beautiful corner posts. Looked gorgeous inside the cabin. You must have seen them in your photographs. But the four points where they connected to the deck made it weak. All you need is one wave to crash funny and hit the boat at one of those joints." Andrew smacks his fist into his palm. "The coach house comes off and you're left with a saucer."

So much water.

"Hell, even the windows on the coach house were dangerous. There were four each on the port and starboard sides and two facing the bow. They brought light into the cabin but...in a storm? I don't know." Andrew looks away from my face as if embarrassed.

"Did you ever talk to David about the boat's design?"

"No. I didn't bring it up."

"You never thought to tell them that *Mugwump* had some weak points?"

"You know what your brother was like. He probably wouldn't have taken it well."

Andrew takes deep draw on his cigarette. "It was a beautiful boat. A good boat."

I'm not sure if he's trying to convince himself or me.

I swallow a large mouthful of beer. My throat doesn't let it down easily. Is it possible that *Mugwump* wasn't built for this kind of sailing, at all?

"Do you think it's crazy, Andrew? Sailing so far in such a small boat?"

"Of course it's mad." Orange firelight flashes in his eyes. "Anyone can see the simple madness of it. Well, anyone with sense can see it. But what's there to do? Dreams don't let go. They're who we are. And they promise something. What? I don't know. Freedom? That's hogwash too. But what the hell. For most of us life's nothing but a blind stumble. You got to love those who make a journey out of it."

"It was freedom David was after, Andrew. Freedom to live exactly as he wanted."

"I know. We had many long shit sessions about that. It was one of his favourite subjects."

"But do you think he might have confused freedom with escapism?"

"Can't say I'd know the answer to that but listen. Your brother was all right, you know? He was brilliant."

"WHAT ARE YOU DRINKING, sweetheart?" David asks me with a Bogart flare.

"Since it's my last night here, how about a scotch?"

"Which one? The top shelf is the expensive stuff—the reserves, the aged, the single malts. Only the tourists will pay that price," he says. "The locals can barely afford the lower shelf except when the dole gets paid out."

"I'm a tourist. Give me one from the top shelf."

"Any one in particular?"

"I'll start on the left and see how far I can go."

I sip fire. I love the feeling in my chest, the burn, the heart pumping an extra beat, fingertips glowing. By my second glass, the limbs are already turning soft and wobbly. So this is why we have knees—to adjust for the rolling floor.

"Drinkin' scotch is like sailing," I tell David after a third. "You gotta keep an eye fixed on the horizon."

I stare at my brother's hand gripping a black-labelled bottle with gold writing. His knuckles are turning pink as if he's clenching too hard. Small moons lift from his fingers, white against the red nail beds. The black label grows until it isn't paper any longer but a darkness that folds over the bar.

HEATHER FINDS ME IN the yard watching the cat stalk something in the long grass.

"My favourite memory of your brother is watching him eat carrots that he just pulled from the garden. He'd wash them under the tap and then lean on that pole." She points to a four-foot-high post where a hose is attached. "He'd stand ever so long just looking over the garden and eating carrots. When I think of him, that's what I see."

I follow her gaze to the cleared field. Only half of it has been planted this year.

"I have some letters you might like to read," she says. She slides a blue airmail letter into my hand. "This one's from Dave. He sent it to me a few months after meeting Sarah. But the rest are hers." She hands me a stack of envelopes held together with an elastic band. No airmail paper for Sarah. She had used real stationery. "You know, I think in almost every one she mentions your brother."

"Thank you, Heather."

"I'll leave you be, then. I'm going in to have a little lie-down."

I watch her duck under the drooping clothesline, heavy with jeans and pink wrinkled towels crushed by the wringer. Her blond hair gets snagged along a frayed edge of cotton, revealing a small band of dark roots. Heather must think of

Sarah every time she crosses this yard. Her daughter's clothes used to hang in this air.

I drag a wobbly lawn chair across the yard and face it away from the house and caravan. I sink into its cradle of woven nylon mesh.

In the garden I see a man in a dark mackintosh sitting on his haunches, boots caked with mud from the night's rain. The lower half of his jacket is marked with hand-swipes of dirt. His head bends over, fingers slipping the thin white roots out of the earth. He inches forward, meticulously weeding. A pearly mist floats along the narrow footpaths between the rows. When he stands up, my brother looks taller than I remember, and broader. His body grows until his shoulders break through the clouds. He's as large as the Scottish giant who walked across the sea using islands as stepping-stones.

"Do you remember the vegetable people we used to make?" I ask him, walking between the rows.

"That was a bizarre and twisted outcome of gardening," says David.

As children we had used toothpicks to hold together potato heads, carrot legs, and green bean arms. Hair was dill, wilted lettuce or carrot tops. I once made a terrible-looking beet hag.

I watch him put a little carrot into his mouth and crunch softly. "I love my garden."

THE ELASTIC BAND SNAPS across the back of my hand as I slide it off the bundle of envelopes. A brief red welt forms. A postcard falls to my lap.

Hi Mum—this is the coastguard station that has our 'small craft safety scheme' card—we're supposed to send this to someone on shore who might be concerned. Anyway you'll hopefully never need it!

I slide the card back under the envelopes.

The first letter I read is one that David wrote to Heather. It's dated July 6, 1988, and mailed from Darwin, Australia. I laugh when I notice that the penmanship is much neater than in the letters I received. The *O*s are round and the *L*s are tall and elliptical. He must have struggled to keep the pen moving smoothly.

There's a few things I must clear up. I'm not always as 'jolly' as I look in the pictures, only when I'm with Sarah. It's hard to be down because Sarah's so up; she has a lust for life that's uncommon (I love it). A trait one assumes she inherited from her mom.

Ah, the sweet charm of a man in love.

Thanks for having such a wonderful daughter (or 4) and I'll take care of her or more like, she'll take care of me.

A letter from Sarah, written a few months earlier, introduces David to her mother.

Anyway—I'll tell you about the type of person Dave is. Well— he's actually pretty similar to me in some ways! Surprisingly so, I mean—we seem to have a lot of some of the same ideas about things—and we get on really well. And we like doing lots of the same things too—I mean he has the same travel urges, loves camping and the outdoors, is really easy-going—oh I can't really give you much of an idea—some facts: he's 28, Canadian, runs marathons (he's done 9) and is really fit. He was working in Canada at the fisheries, helping in the lab with genetics research work on fish, and—a bit like me—the govt. money ran out. He has a degree in General Science—part of which was Geology, but mostly Biology, but then got a job selling Campbell's soups!

In April, she wrote,

Hey—me and Dave are getting on so well, I can't really explain it—I'm very happy! We have loads of plans for travelling all over the world and that includes Mull of course, so I hope you like him!

In June, she gushes, *I've never been this much in love before.*

I flip through the cancel dates in the right hand corner of the envelopes.

Heather received letters regularly, sometimes every week. The most recent correspondence from Sarah include details of their life on *Mugwump*: the difficulty in acquiring sailing charts in small Irish towns, the state of the winds, the problems with the boat, and David's Middle Eastern cuisine cooked on a camping stove. Sarah writes sparingly about her feelings and fears, but she does provide a glimpse of her life with my brother. Her sense of humour is evident and probably well needed.

Lots of other (minor) things keep happening too, but the basic pattern of events is the same—piece of equipment fails, Dave gets extremely annoyed, Sarah doesn't get too worried at first because she's got such faith in Dave fixing it, Dave gets increasingly and more volubly annoyed as he tries to fix it, Sarah gets increasingly worried and tries, rather in vain, to cheer Dave up and look on the bright side, which usually involves making stupid suggestions. (If these are stupid enough they'll actually make Dave

*laugh, but occasionally they get him at least thinking along dif-
ferent lines . . . .) Finally, Dave fixes the offending item and all is
well again.*

Sarah's last letter was mailed August 31, 1995 from
Castletownbere. It probably took four or five days to reach
Heather. It is possible they had already perished by the time
these words were read.

*Thursday, August 24, 1995
Broadhaven Bay, County Mayo*

Hi Mum,

> *As you'll see from the postmark, we've had to make a stop
here in Ireland. Unless our progress improves dramatically we'll
probably have to give the Azores a miss and head straight for
Madeira. It does seem that in the past week we've met problem
after problem.*

> *You'll have heard from Andrew we didn't get off Thursday
till late afternoon. We had to rebuild the bilge pump. By that time
the fair wind of earlier that day had all but died, and we were feeling pretty thwarted, when Andrew came and cheered us up! It was
great to have a 'traditional" sending off by another yacht. We took
a couple of pictures of Sequina under sail, which I'll send back
for Andrew if they're good.*

> *Anyway, since fixing the bilge pump, that's been okay—we've
coped with dead batteries, temperamental log, and what we thought
was VHF failure but turned out to be low battery. We can't understand the batteries, which kept their charges fine while we were at
the boatyard—now we've disconnected the older one—perhaps it's
draining the other—a new (well 1 year old now) deep cycle marine
battery (over £80 worth!), it MUST be ok!*

The latest thing though, as we sped along with a fair NW wind at last, but put on the engine to recharge the battery, was like adding insult to injury—it started to cut out! Dave tried a few things on the move but we got to a decision point and had to head into Broadhaven Bay—the only safe easy-to-get-into haven for a long while.

It was lucky we did. What we thought at first would be a couple of hours fixing, turned into the rest of the day, without a diagnosis. . . . Dave couldn't find anything wrong. Eventually, after completely exhausting numerous theories and tests, it was with heavy hearts we rowed ashore the next afternoon.

In fact, our trip into Belmullet was a huge success. We found a great bloke who came out to the boat the same day, worked with Dave on it for a couple of hours and would only take a fiver in return!

Anyway, now we're stuck in Broadhaven Bay for at least another day while these gale-force SW winds blow! It's a lovely spot and we've been enjoying reading, writing, Scrabble, cooking. Sailing continuously through the night and getting our sleep in 2–3 hour shifts has left us needing a bit of a rest anyway.

Anyway, we've kept getting to stages over the last 2 weeks thinking 'NOW we're ready . . . !' but it really does seem like we are now! As long as we have a break from these strong Swesterleys before too long.

I'll leave some space to write just before I go to the P.O., wherever that may be . . . .

Hi! After two fantastic days of sailing with a fair wind, here we are in Castletownbere! We set off midday Monday and anchored here 5:30 a.m. this morning, Wednesday. There were still two more layers of problems related to the engine after I wrote!—so we missed the start of the good winds but never mind here we are *now! Hopefully a day of stocking up, doing laundry and showers and then—next stop Madeira! There's a huge high over us now—we just made it here in time before the winds fell light— so it's a gorgeous bright sunny day; waking up this morning after a few hours sleep it felt like we could already be in Madeira!*

    Speak to you soon.

    Love Sarah xox

I fold the stiff letter paper along its crease.

    Problem after problem

    Rebuild the bilge pump

I slide the elastic over the envelopes and carry the bundle to the trailer.

    Temperamental log

    VHF failure

I put them on the table.

    Dead batteries

    Two more layers of problems related to the engine

The wind catches the caravan door and slams it into the side.

They threw away their lives.

    The problems that were so obvious, after the fact, had been glossed over by two people who wouldn't recognize the reality of their situation.

    Mugwump's equipment was inferior. She wasn't nearly ready to make a sea voyage of 1,200 miles.

I FILL THE KETTLE with water, thinking tea will calm me, but the rumble of the water makes me angry. I turn off the burner and go outside. I see my ten-speed bike leaning against a wall. I forgot it was here. I gave the bike to David when he was in Canada with Sarah. He had enthusiastically made a plan to arrive at his new home in Fionnphort pedalling under his own steam. David was adamant when he explained his thinking. "This is not just about personal power and freedom. It's about our addiction to gas-powered transportation." But the day the ferry dropped him and Sarah at Craignure, it was raining so hard, he abandoned the idea and took the bus.

Why couldn't you have done that again, David? Had a change of heart at the last minute.

Another winter in England or Scotland? David answers in my head. *That sounded so dismal Sarah and I never gave it much thought. Onward! we yelled and laughed. To sea! And come what may! Weather is impossible to predict, as everyone knows, and boats, too, it turns out. In fact, all of it is unknowable. Even Sarah and myself. We were armed with fibreglass and metal, cotton sails and tough skins. And of course, our wills, such as they were. We dared fate like everyone else. And why not success? We took our chance.*

You're right. So much is unknowable except for two variables: you and Sarah. Self-reflection is the gift that combats the great unknown. The two of you had enough information to critically analyze the situation, take into account personal goals, and then consider the impact of such a decision. What was your life worth to you?

Did you think returning to England and having to work all winter to make enough money to replace the piece-of-shit engine, would have been demoralizing? Would your personal myth be shattered? Being careful and patient has never been your habit. Postponing the voyage may have forced you to view yourself as a man with a little less style, less bravado. But you might still be alive and there wouldn't be all these confused people mourning for you and Sarah.

We haven't known what to think. We don't know how angry we can be. Can we be furious at circumstance, or should we express our rage at you? For once we would have liked you to lead with your head. We wanted you to be detached, doubtful, resolute in your evaluation of *Mugwump's* suitability. More like Dad, the time he talked you into coming home when you ran away. *Take your time,* he said. *There's no rush, David. We'll see you when you get here.*

Why did you always have to push so hard?

What exactly were you trying to prove, again? That mediocrity was worse than death?

It was a stupid to leave port in Ireland. It wasn't brave or philosophical or daring. You cut your life so short you missed out on a thousand other thrills.

It was my choice.

It was the wrong one, David.

My body shakes as I try to put the elastic around the letters.

Heather crosses the yard with a basket of laundry.

She smiles at me.

I'm sorry, Heather.

How is she not furious?

ON FRIDAY EVENING, SARAH's father walks in the door of Heather and Derek's house, grabs my hands and says, "My God, you look just like him." I cry and he cries, too, hugging me so hard my bones hurt. Later at dinner, he gives a speech, his voice halting, trembling. "I am angry at the sea for taking two, beautiful, intelligent people when there are so many others left not worth half their existence."

At dinner, I feel Sarah's absence. This is a family of four girls and now the eldest is gone. Rachel, the sister born after

Sarah, reminds me of glass, not its fragility, just some quality that catches and reflects light. She hugs me often, or just reaches out and grabs my hand. Zoë, the youngest, has come from London. She talks to the cat in the kitchen, a long conversation about what the feline has seen on an afternoon walk across the fields. At first I thought grief had touched her only lightly, just skimming across the surface like a flat pebble, but I've noticed when she is sitting quietly, there is a small shudder caught under her skin. "You never know when you're going to feel it," she says to me. "That wave of unbearable sadness."

But it is Xanthe, the third-born daughter, Sarah's best friend, who suffers openly.

"The worst thing about this is not the not knowing," she says, "but the fact that they are gone. My own life has been made smaller." She slips her hands into the dishwater and in slow circles washes a white plate. "I feel better after I've cried. But ultimately, we're crying for ourselves."

I pick up a tea towel and wipe the china dry.

"I know you didn't get a chance to see Sarah and Dave with *Mugwump*, but they were so confident," says Xanthe. "Regardless of what others thought about their skill, this was the right thing for them. I will never believe that they made the wrong decision."

"But they're not here, Xanthe. Some part of this *was* wrong." My voice is loud.

Derek looks at me. My resolve to be contained is wavering. The argument I have been having with David since I read the letters wants to escape into Heather's kitchen. If my brother had realistically assessed *Mugwump's* problems he would have concluded that the boat wasn't seaworthy for such a long journey. There were too many occurrences of problems in a short period of time. A lack of experience in sailing on open seas should have been another consideration, as Sam had tried to tell me almost a year ago. And though Sarah and David likely made the decision together, there is only one captain on a boat. David should have aborted the voyage. And perhaps Sarah shouldn't have loved him so much.

I bite my tongue and vigorously polish a dinner knife.

Matt, Rachel's fiancé, who has been sitting at the table, enters the conversation. "If there was anyone with whom I would trust my life, it would have been Dave," he says, taking a sip of red wine from a large glass. Matt is a confident man. He expects people to trust in him too.

"And Dave had changed," says Richard, Xanthe's partner. "When we first met him in Japan, he would never let up in a discussion. He was convinced he was always right. But later, after he moved here, he relaxed. He let other people's views in, he listened to other perspectives."

No one wants to speak ill of the dead.

Is it because I am here?

Or do they truly believe that David and Sarah acted wisely?

After the dishes are done, Richard sets up the slide projector. David and Sarah had taken hundreds of photographs while travelling through Asia. We go through the pictures slowly. No one speaks. The machine clicks, the fan whirs in the silence. David and Sarah are smiling at us. Lint on the projector sometimes pockmarks their faces or adds a skewed moustache. We laugh when David is doing something silly, making a face, wrestling with Sarah. He manipulates his body in each photo—a leg stretched at an odd angle, an arm draped casually over Sarah's shoulder. He never seems to be standing still. And while Sarah is always looking right at the camera, David is often caught glancing out of the frame.

Click. Sarah is straddling a black one-gear bicycle. Behind her, a blur of wheels and bodies—the grey-dressed Chinese commuting through Guangzhou in a throng as tight as a peloton.

Click. David is holding a candle over a bowl of rice on his thirty-first birthday.

Click. Sarah and David are standing unusually solemn in front of the rebuilt Golden Pavilion in Kyoto. I know this photo. David liked the story of how a young monk, obsessed with the beauty of the three-tiered temple, lit it on fire and watched it go up in flames. *You always destroy what you love,* David had quoted to me in a letter.

I close my eyes. Madras, Beijing, Tokyo. Sarah always smiling.

Click. Sarah under a palm tree with a drink in her hand.

"Look how tanned she is," someone says.

"I can practically hear the ice tinkling." Some laughter.

Richard leaves the slide on the wall for a long time. We all want her to be in the room with us.

I look around at the faces dimly lit by the projector's bulb. Sarah's family stares calmly at the palm fronds bending with a breeze but my heart sinks with a terrible thought.

He killed her.

David didn't protect Sarah from himself.

After the slide machine has cooled and returned to its box, I retreat to the caravan. I fold the table down and make up the bed. I pull the duvet around my neck but I can't get warm. My body shivers uncontrollably like it's trying to shake something off.

Sarah's sisters and their partners walk by the caravan on the way down to Bull Hole for an icy swim. Their drunken laughter floats through the open window. I recognize Richard's voice.

"You're right to look at everything, consider every possibility," he had said to me after the slide show. "There's a peace that can come from that kind of examination. But in the end it doesn't matter. It's over." He put his hand on my shoulder. "We have to stop being so sad for them. They made a choice. No one could have stopped them."

I thought I knew my brother. In fact, only a year ago, I believed that I was the *only* one who really understood David. I had him figured out. He was passionate but not stupid. He had personal principles but wasn't reckless. But how do I view him now? With pity? He would hate that more than anything. He'd rather be seen as a fool.

Last fall, when I realized that I couldn't save David, I decided to define him. I vowed to follow the threads of his life and see why events had unfolded as they did. Could I unearth David's character, reveal a poetic soul, and announce that he had not died in vain? Perhaps this is a common thing that siblings do—struggle to make sense of a sister or a brother who is gone.

What I failed to understand though was how much of myself I had vested in David's character. Something had happened when David and I were in our late twenties. He started travelling just when I stopped. I settled down and he picked up the thread and ran with it. In fact, he had the true wanderlust. I knew I would never trade my family for his life but I could support what I could no longer have and sometimes longed for. I would live vicariously through him. And I would never judge

There is something else that I didn't understand. I had made a claim to a life that wasn't my own. David's search for freedom and meaning wasn't mine. My unfulfilled life could not be lived through him.

David did not belong to me. He was not *my* brother exclusively. I was not the only one who knew him and I was not the only one who loved him deeply. It wasn't just up to me to save him. Or protect him. Or hold him back. Or lead the way. We were all involved. My family. Sarah's family. Their friends. We all share in the responsibility for the lives of those we love.

I WAKE FROM A dream with the scent of propane in my nose.

Soft light is floating under the scallop-edged curtains.

Sam's voice repeats in my head, *You'll never be happy.* And then he walks out the front door of our house, taking the kitchen table with him.

Where are you going? Are you coming back, Sam?

He stops but doesn't turn around. He bends his knees and readjusts the glass top tucked under one arm while hiking up the four-legged metal frame under the other.

You're leaving me without a table?

But that's where I waited for David's call. That's where I charted *Mugwump's* voyage. Over a map of an island, I eat meals with my children at that table.

Sam walks down the street, the poplar trees casting yellow shadows across his back. *It was my grandmother's,* he says, reading my thoughts, as one can in a dream. *And now it's mine.*

I throw back the quilt and sit on the edge of the bed. I am short of breath.

A small white feather that has worked its spiny point through the cotton duvet floats in the grey light.

Cold linoleum sends small shock waves through my feet.

You'll never be happy.

Without standing up I strike a match and light the burner. I place the kettle over the flames and stare into a pool of metal. A small dent in the aluminum reflects my image like a miniature picture frame—my face contorts as I move my head back and forth.

Never.

When the kettle whistles I pour the steaming water into the teapot and toss two mesh bags on the surface. They float for a moment and then sink.

I tried to call Sam yesterday after reading Sarah's letters but I couldn't get through. I was angry and I wanted to tell him that my brother may have killed Sarah with ambition and selfishness. *He killed her like you're killing me, Sam,* I imagined saying. *I am sinking under your dream.*

But now, in the morning's soft light, sitting on this narrow little bed in a caravan on the top of a hill, I see it differently. There are choices we make for ourselves and there are choices that others make for us. We must know the difference.

I convert the bed back into a table and two benches, and gather the feather duvet into my arms. I push the quilt through the narrow opening, the door slamming against the outside wall of the caravan. In the yard, one clothesline is already sagging with pants and shirts so I throw a corner of the duvet over the second line. I tug at it from the other side until a rectangle of white hangs evenly like a letter envelope. But now, both clotheslines are full and there is no room if Heather has laundry. I carry the duvet back to the trailer and attempt to stuff it into the wheel well under one of the bench seats. Each time I give it a punch, a small stitched pocket of cotton rises with trapped air. It reminds me of another moment—*Lady Papillon's* spinnaker sail still holding the wind.

When I finally get the quilt enclosed in the compartment I sit on the lid and wait for the air to dissipate. The yellow spinnaker hadn't wanted to be put away either. It had tumbled onto my head in the fore cabin and refused to be stuffed into its sail bag. It rippled at my feet as if reminding me that it wanted to return to air and fly ahead of us, pulling and lifting, hull and hearts together.

The spinnaker was an idea and we were to chase it.

The sail is a transcendent metaphor.

No wonder some are called to its beauty and function. It is our imagination carrying us into the unknown. It is our physical body, the skin rising up, daring to be a force that would equal the wind.

It is also the self.

Receiving and expanding. Moving freely throughout the world.

If we dared to peel back the flesh of our limitations, smoothing out every scar and wrinkle—those lasting remnants of our fears—would the wind fly us translucent into the sky? Would we follow beauty and truth the way we see it? Would the world fill us with its own dreams?

And finally, could we live the invisible stories, no longer fearing our uncertain lives?

IONA

Freedom is not a philosophy, nor is it even an idea.
It is a movement of consciousness that leads, at certain
moments, to utter one of two monosyllables: Yes or No. In
their brevity, lasting but an instant, like a flash of lightning,
the contradictory character of human nature stands revealed.

OCTAVIO PAZ

THE SOUND OF IONA is calm this morning. There's not a ripple
on the narrow channel, only a soft rain mottling the water's surface. I lean over the ferry railing and watch the grey skin of the
sea sweep under the bow-like silk stitched by a needle. Through
the rain I can just make out the yellow shore and the soft green
hills. Iona emerges from the mist like a polished stone.

The *M. V. Loch Buie* docks at Baile Mór, a single-street village of high-peaked houses that faces the sea. I walk down the

ramp, give a wave to a friend of David's who's at the ferry's helm today, and cross the wooden jetty. Instead of following the crowd heading for the Abbey, I take the tarmac road leading south to a wide beach of pale sand. The morning's low tide exposes a deep strand studded with black volcanic rocks. The rocks resemble sleeping seals. Or the dark heads of sailors washed up on shore.

I have been here before. A blue-sky day in May, three years ago. David, Sarah, and I had stopped to look east across these waters to the hills of Mull. David pointed out the pink granite cliffs, the peak of Ben Mor, and then he directed my gaze to a small rise of land. On its lee side, hidden from our view, was the blue and white caravan he and Sarah called home.

I EMPTY THE DRAWERS under the sofa first.

There isn't much to recover. The true wanderer doesn't keep many material possessions for fear it will tie him down, but some things remain, the basic elements of a life. There is paper: books of poetry, travel, geology, and five small diaries. There is wool: sweaters folded in fourths, the arms crossed, or stretched beyond recognition. There is plastic: a mangled toothbrush, bristles that once rubbed against soft red gums. And there is wood: a model sailboat David built without a kit. I balance the balsa hull in my hand. How light. It would need ballast in the keel to stay upright. And the mast is too short, it wants another third of length. I put the items into a box, tape it shut and write my parent's address on the front. Other than the diaries and the juggling balls, it all will go to them. By surface mail, it will take three months to get to Winnipeg.

I am almost ready to go home. To return to the birthdays that need celebrating and the grief that must be faced. And there is more, something still unnamed. Something barely understood. A yearning for more life has been awakened in me. Perhaps this is what David has been saying to me all along: real desire is rooted in curiosity and uncertainty.

I have learned something else too. There are times in our lives when we need pushing. And times when we need protection from ourselves. From our dreams, desires, choices, ideas, our habits. We need someone to say, *No*. We need someone to say, *Yes*. We need someone to not abandon us when we are weak or blind or selfish.

I will be leaving my brother here on the Scottish islands that soothed his fiery temperament and inspired him to resurrect his boyhood dream.

I will miss him. David has been with me every day for the last year. We kept hold of each other like two lost children, and never let go. I carried him with me wherever I travelled and perhaps in some strange working of the spirit I did find him on the shores of Madeira and have returned him here. To Mull. To Iona, this ancient, holy island.

I have just enough time today to take a walk with him and Sarah. I will follow them in a slow circle around the island. Sarah in a blue jacket. David in yellow. We'll wander the same route as three years before, our footprints already here. Memories will lead like a pale hand.

I open the map I purchased from the Ferry Shop in Fionnphort and hold it in front of me. Every bay, meadow, hillock, mound, pasture, gully, strand, cliff, and rock outcropping is labelled in Gaelic and English. *Iomair Cha'n Iomair Sgeir* is Row You Can't Row Skerry. *Port Lobha* is the Port of Rotting. *Uiridh nam Braonan* is Bed of the Earthnuts. I imagine the translations as titles of poems. I head for *Blar nam Manach*, the Plain of the Monks, and follow a path across some machair. My feet press into the short springy turf that grows on a base of sand. It reminds me of walking in the great cedar and hemlock forests on the coast of British Columbia. The earth receives your weight like a lover and you want to sink into it.

There are no forests on Iona. The land is bare, stripped by the wind and a long history of habitation. I am the tallest thing and closest to the sky as I walk over the moor towards *Cnoc Mor Nan Gall*, Big Hill of the Strangers. At the top of the hill, I see the grey ocean, round and rippled like a ball of wool. I have stood here, before, with David and Sarah, our eyes searching for the Dhu Heartach Lighthouse that floats between sea and sky on the rocks near Torran Reef. David had pointed to the warning beacon flashing on the horizon like a slow pulsing star. Ireland was just on the other side of the sea's bulge, one hundred miles to the southwest, a twenty-four-hour sail in a small boat.

From my pocket, I take out David's red diary. I have been carrying the book inside my jacket since I found it, reading the short entries while sitting on rocks, beaches, ferry docks, and now hilltops. David had abruptly stopped writing in an earlier diary and began this one just three days after he first kissed Sarah on a beach in Australia. I like to imagine these words as the beginning of their story.

Walked up the coast. Beautiful vistas but all I could see is Sarah. Stopped by a small stream, took a skinny dip in a deep pool. Poured water over each other. Spent the night making slow beautiful love. That night lay out under the stars wondering what the night will bring.

From *Sithean Mor na h'Aird*, Big Fairy Mound of the Aird, I slip down a gully carved into a small cove on the southeast coast of the island. Hand over foot, I climb over the boulders of an abandoned marble quarry. It's been eighty years since the last block of marble was carried away across the sound to Mull. All that is left is the iron skeleton of an old conveying system rusting in the salt air.

At the shore I plunge my hands into the shallows searching for an egg-shaped rock. The colour drains until my skin is pale. Two white birds flutter under the surface. The heavy silt sucks at my fingers and wrists, and I am drawn downward.

ON OUR KNEES, DAVID and I claw in the flooding hollows, stirring the water grey until we find what we are looking for.

"Let's see," says Sarah, appearing beside us. I open my hand to her, still stiff with the memory of ice water. In my palm rests a small white stone laced with ribbons of pale green. "It's called nephrite. It was once limestone."

"What turns it green?" I ask, rubbing the stone, its surface smooth as soap.

"Chemistry. Heat and pressure. The minerals in the rock collapse into each other."

"Isn't that geology degree handy?" David teases her. His hand grips her shoulder as he stands up. His feet sink into the pebbles. "What else do you know, Professor?"

"I know that Iona has some of the oldest rock in the world. A history spanning a few thousand million years."

"Or so," David adds and laughs.

"Mull's a volcanic baby in comparison. Iona has evidence of very early life. There may be good reason the island is considered holy."

"I thought it was because of Druids and Christians," I say.

"Yes, but maybe it all began with rock. The marble on this island is considered special. Fishermen believed it protected them from storms at sea. That's why the old altar in the Abbey had chipped corners. And there are some who think the Coronation Stone in Westminster Abbey actually came from Iona. According to legend, the Druids called it 'The Black Stone of Destiny.'"

"An unbeatable combination," says David. "The power of religion and nature."

I clutch my stone. Its temperature defies its hot, turbulent beginnings and yet there is a hint of its future uses: sepulchres, tombs, altars, statues—the cold and enduring forms for art, ritual, and death.

"If you think about it," says Sarah, "it's amazing how forms on earth change over time. Earthquakes create islands. Sand is squeezed into rock. Crystals are made from fire. Even a shell or a tiny sea creature can become something different altogether. Like a marble egg."

Sarah crouches down and gathers some stones into her hand. She throws them, one at a time into the sound, marking the sea's surface with small explosions of white spray. The wind ruffles her short burnished hair and flattens the blue jacket against her back. Her shadow falls into a hollowed rock filled with seawater—a tidal pool of delicate life.

There are lessons in geology. Everything once alive is transformed. Heated, crushed, folded, split apart, forced together. All endures. Love too.

I will never get tired of talking to her, David wrote in his diary.

Under the earth, wild molecules are dancing.

IONA IS SMALL. JUST three miles long and one-and-a-half wide. The worn pathways of cattle and pilgrims twist across the damp moors and allow for slow meandering.

From the rise of *Cnoc Cul ri Eirinn,* The Hill of Turning the Back to Ireland, I make my way down to a wide plain of pebbles. The water slaps lazily on the sloping shoreline. Stones, coloured like red and green turtles, roll back and forth, clattering in the surf. I bury myself in the pebbles and listen to the soft melody of the sea, a litany of measured waves answering the wind. A musician or a priest could find a song amongst this scattering of notes.

My map tells me that the bay is called *Port a' Churiach,* Harbour of the Coracle. This is the place where in 563 A.D. an Irish priest named Columba fell to his knees and vowed to never return to his homeland. The priest was a renowned scribe in Ireland but when he made an unauthorized copy of a new Latin version of the Bible called the Vulgate, the High King of Ireland demanded that he give it up. "To every cow its calf, and to every book its copy." Columba refused. The great Battle of Cul Dremne followed in which three thousand men were killed over a violation of copyright. Although Columba and his supporters were the victors, Columba was distraught by the bloodshed and banished himself to the eastern lands that lay over the sea. He set out in a wooden, hide-covered boat with twelve clansmen—a refugee seeking penance for his sin of stubbornness.

I wonder if it's the same for everyone who dares to live the adventuring life? Kneeling on a shore, thin as the edge of consciousness, preparing to seek what at first one can only imagine: the mystery of the expanding self. Making the wish that every sailor utters in blind, dark faith—*Let us begin and not falter*—and setting upon the water with rigging taut and hopeful sails, a singular journey for one's own Ithaca.

I am one of the multitudes born to human parents, David writes. *But, I've not yet surrendered to the force of gravity, that universal immoveable demon. I seek to escape this human form and fly—to see how the world really looks in context to the stars.*

He could not do it alone. He needed the wind. He needed Sarah.

THE AFTERNOON SUN MAKES a brief appearance and the island's colours come to life. Verdant green machair lit like green glass. Clusters of harebells tossing bright lavender caps in the wind. On the rise of a small hill, an ochre field of long grass bends softly like Manitoba barley. Even the small-headed daisies glow white in the meadows as I walk through the fields, closing gates behind me.

The highest point on the island is *Dûn-I*, Hill Fort of Iona.

I leave the road leading to the Abbey and pick out a path up a steep, rocky slope. Grazing black-faced sheep watch my progress. When I reach the top, the marbled waters of the Sea of Hebrides hold my gaze. Under angled shafts of dust-laden sunlight, the landfalls of islands swirl blue and green. Tiree and Coll lie low along the horizon. In front of them, Dutchman's Cap and Lunga float like forgotten hats. To the north, I see the faint rising of Staffa, the famous basalt-pillared island visited by Keats, Wordsworth, Tennyson. Three years ago, I climbed over Staffa's stepped black columns of cooled lava and stood in Fingal's Cave. Sarah and I listened to David throw his voice in the sea-formed cathedral that inspired Mendelssohn's *Hebrides Overture*. Against the cavern walls, the tide counted out its timeless tempo while David held three notes: *FI-GA-RO!* Sarah had visibly trembled. David took her hand and led her out of the cave.

The Abbey of Iona sits alone in a pasture. The wide blue band of the Iona Sound sweeps behind. Pink granite walls glow in the sunlight. I return to the road and fall in line with pilgrims making their way to the Cathedral. We follow the Street of the Dead, where the real Macbeth and fifty other Kings of Scotland are buried. We pass by St. Oran's Chapel and I recall the gruesome legend of the monk who was buried alive.

The story goes that Columba, unable to keep the walls of the chapel from falling down every night, had to ask for a volunteer to satisfy a local pagan tradition. Oran, willing to be sacrificed, was interred under the rock foundation. The walls stood firm. But three days later, Columba was in such deep grief for his friend he had the monk's face uncovered. Oran's pale lips uttered the blasphemous words: "Heaven is not as it has been written; neither is hell as commonly supposed." Columba called to the other monks, "Earth, earth in the mouth of Oran, so that he may blab no more," silencing the voice that would speak of what lay beyond death, and under stone.

I climb the small steps leading up to the Cathedral and pause to admire the structure first constructed in the twelfth century by Benedictine monks. Columba's original monastery made of wood and wattle was destroyed two hundred years earlier. Up close the granite is variegated, hues of soft peach and grey, speckled with silver mica. I put my hand on the stone. It's still warm though the clouds have erased the sun.

Behind me, an excited tour group gathers, shaking and snapping umbrellas though there has been little rain since morning. They are anxious to enter, and I am pushed forward by hands and elbows pressing into my back. We tumble into the nave like a multi-limbed beast, shuffling down the centre aisle until I break away and retreat down a narrow row of wooden chairs. The animal moves on, barely slowing to admire the saints in the stained glass windows before going in search of the cloisters.

I lift a hymnbook from a seat and sit down. My eye is drawn upward to the pointed arches that divide the church into antechambers: the nave and tower, the choir and transepts, and finally the chapel at the far end where a leaded-glass window blazes white like a directed searchlight. The air is heavy with ashen dust motes.

I follow no faith, though various churches floated in and out of my childhood, but today I long for the language and poetry of a religious service. Words of praise and forgiveness. A hymn I might recognize. A parable. I cast my eyes over the empty chairs, imagining the expectant expressions of a congregation. Faces open with lifted eyes. Waiting for a voice to call our souls in from the wilderness.

We are strangers before Christ, a white-robed shadow at the pulpit announces, *brought together in this place of prayer.* My head lowers, fingers press, the almond-tipped shape of the architecture repeats in my hands.

Today we honour the lives of two adventurers.

Who has heard the old story about a sailor who left shore to seek the soul?

David Ostlere and Sarah Heald were lost at sea in September 1995. Never reaching their destination, they disappeared without a trace.

Into the deep, Jonah cried. You threw me into the heart of the sea.

We are all joined to Christ's sacrifice and receive its inexhaustible benefits.

Our Father, who art in Heaven....

We remember their families.

Shore us up, in our darkness.
The Lord be with you.
And with thy spirit.
Lift up your hearts.
O' crumbled muscles. We lift them up unto eternity.

I LEAVE THE ABBEY and walk to the north end of Iona where the beaches are long and wide. Along the shoreline the tide has etched its retreat like a lined hand. I spread my jacket across the sand and sit at the edge of the water. According to the map, immediately in front of me is *Eilean Annraidh*, Island of Storm, a land mass made of little more than a cluster of pointed rocks erupting like knife-edge keels. The ocean and wind will spend years smoothing these pinnacles.

I take David's diary from my pocket and open it on my lap. The gold-edged pages glint even though the sun has faded.

Stayed tonite at Bundeena. A beautiful night of sweet, soft touching. Caught the ferry to Cronella then the train. Now I'm on my way to the future in Sarah's hands and I love it!

I like these words. David's earliest declaration of his own fate. He chose Sarah. She chose him. And now the future could begin. David is the ardent *other* who will show Sarah a disappearing vision: a world where an individual can search for freedom. Sarah is the goddess on David's shoulder, breathing into his ear, *I will go with you so you are not alone.* They whisper to each other, *Wake up now, I'm here.*

Along the horizon, flashes of lightning burn the sky and illuminate a long grey ruffle of gathering clouds. I wait for the thunder, counting like a child, and not taking a breath until it arrives. The sound rolls in on wooden wheels. Under the echoes, I imagine a sea rising—rows of rippled marching swells, the broken white crests of mounting waves, and between them, the silent troughs, the slide to oblivion and out.

The wind reaches Iona's shore and stirs the air. Small vortexes dance along the tops of dunes. A gull feather pinwheels down the beach. The marram grass bends and rustles as if a lost prairie breeze has found its way here. I close my eyes against a curtain of sand-filled air and see *Mugwump* sailing across a golden field. She heels to starboard. A field of grain parts under her keel, soughing and murmuring. On her deck, my brother winches the mainsail. The canvas tightens like a skin, bulging with blue sky.

Perhaps the boat was always there, sailing across a glacier-carved plain, waiting for a boy to dream it and carry him to sea. The teenager turns the pages of an atlas in his bedroom. He glances at a poster of a yacht in full sail. He is keeping his dream next to his fears, close by and secret, underground in the basement of a bungalow. He is waiting for when it will all begin: the right country, the proper ocean, a woman, an island, and then he will spill, all of himself—the child, the boy, the man—pouring his life into her. Into Sarah. For she is the cave, the well, the hollow at the bottom of a tree, the space between a jumble of seeds in a flower's cup. Sarah is the shell and the crack in the earth's yielding crust. Inside her body, he learns that love is heat, altering composition and history.

I open my eyes and see a red stone rolling up the sand on the tip of a wave. I pluck it from the water and hold it in my open palm. The water has deepened its colour. The wind dries it pink in my hand. I remember what Sarah said about the Abbey's granite masonry. *The stone has kept the colour of its beginnings. Like an ancient fire still burning.*

Is this true of the human soul as well? If the earth can reveal its metamorphosis in a single rock, what does one life show of the history of humanity? The unquenchable desire to live in freedom? The need to respond to a call from the wild: Come, test your strength and fear? Or the necessity of crossing boundaries, again and again?

I want to believe every soul is carried in the hearts and on the backs of such individuals. Where we dare not go, they go for us. They remind us that the world's first dream was *Life* and they are committed to touching the power of that sacrament.

DAVID AND I ARE standing on the edge of a shore. We are teenagers wheeling stone after stone across the water. The lake is crosshatched like a spider's web. We squint our eyes and follow the bursting circles.

"Now watch me," my younger brother demands.

"I'm watching."

"Bend the knees. Keep your eyes low but look across the water, as far as you can see. Then, pull your shoulder back, keep the elbow high and fling the stone straight at the horizon. And count."

One...two...five...eight....

He always skips the farthest. Or else his eyesight is better. David claims to see the briefest of taps, mere fingerprints grazing the water. *Ten...eleven.*

"You try," he says. "Hold your breath and let it fly. Imagine the stone touching the blue like a whisper and going forever."

Two...four...seven...nine....

I throw better with David at my side.

...twelve...thirteen.

"Now, breathe out," he reminds me.

I rub the Iona stone between my fingers, warming the smooth granite. It's not a good skipper. Too round. No edge to slice through the water. I won't be able to count to three before it sinks. But it's worth keeping anyway. Until I find a better one.

I slide the stone into my pocket and head for the ferry.